DEVELOPING
GODLY
CHARACTER

→·INTENSIVE DISCIPLESHIP COURSE·←

DEVELOPING
GODLY
CHARACTER

VINNIE CARAFANO

YWAM
PUBLISHING
P.O. BOX 55787   SEATTLE, WA 98155

YWAM Publishing is the publishing ministry of Youth With A Mission. Youth With A Mission (YWAM) is an international missionary organization of Christians from many denominations dedicated to presenting Jesus Christ to this generation. To this end, YWAM has focused its efforts in three main areas: (1) training and equipping believers for their part in fulfilling the Great Commission (Matthew 28:19), (2) personal evangelism, and (3) mercy ministry (medical and relief work).

For a free catalog of books and materials, contact
YWAM Publishing
P.O. Box 55787, Seattle, WA 98155
(425) 771-1153 or (800) 922-2143
www.ywampublishing.com

Intensive Discipleship Course: Developing Godly Character
Copyright © 2007 by Vinnie Carafano
King's Kids El Paso
936 Sunset Rd.
El Paso, TX 79922-2149
Ph. (915) 591-8234; Fax (915) 581-1370
carafano@juno.com
www.kkep.org

12 11 10 09 08 07   10 9 8 7 6 5 4 3 2 1

Published by YWAM Publishing
P.O. Box 55787
Seattle, WA 98155

ISBN-10: 1-57658-410-0
ISBN-13: 978-1-57658-410-1

Library of Congress Cataloging-in-Publication Data

Carafano, Vinnie.
    Intensive discipleship course : developing godly character / by Vinnie Carafano.
       p. cm.
    ISBN-13: 978-1-57658-410-1 (pbk.)
    ISBN-10: 1-57658-410-0 (pbk.)
    1. Discipling (Christianity) 2. Spiritual formation. I. Title.
    BV4520.C295 2007
    248.8'3—dc22
                             2007010479

The Scripture quotations in this publication are from the New King James Version. Copyright © 1979, 1980, 1982, Thomas Nelson, Inc

All names in the stories told in the Intensive Discipleship Course: Developing Godly Character have been changed.

Printed in the United States of America

Special thanks to faithful friends and prayer warriors.

CONTENTS

12 WEEKS OF CHALLENGE

RESOURCES

FOREWORD

God has repeatedly called on teenagers throughout history to provide righteous, courageous leadership that has saved the people from destruction. The Intensive Discipleship Course materials provide a biblically based means to effectively equip the Davids and Esthers of our time, reinforcing their capacity to overcome today's giants and extend the kingdom of God throughout their communities and nations.

I deeply appreciate the diligence, wisdom, and sensitivity with which Vinnie and Jodie Carafano have faithfully invested in many young people for the past twenty-seven years in the context of local churches, mission outreaches, and communities at large. One of the main reasons for the Carafanos' effectiveness has been the strong biblical foundations they have been instrumental in nurturing within young lives. This, together with their understanding of how to help young people develop life disciplines that integrate these dynamic truths into all of life, provides an experience-rich backdrop, making the Intensive Discipleship Course series a particularly valuable training resource for any Christian youth worker, teacher, pastor, or parent.

May those who use these materials discover time-tested keys to unlocking the God-intended potential of their youth.

DALE KAUFFMAN
King's Kids International, Founder and President

What Is the Intensive Discipleship Course?

How the Course Began

From 1980 to 1994 I was the youth pastor in a large nondenominational church. In 1986 I realized that it was impossible to give one message at our high-school and college-age group that would meet the needs of all the different kinds of people who came. We had totally devoted, radically sold-out, on-fire, holy, dynamic, soul-winning kids, but we also had unsaved, doing-drugs, criminal-record, topless-dancer, drive-by-shooting-gang-member, Satan-worshiping, lost kids. Then there were those kids in the middle. How in the world

could I present a message from the Word that could affect everyone there?

Most youth groups face the same dilemma. I developed this course to meet the needs of Christian students in high school and college who have a desire to grow in their relationship with the Lord and who need more in-depth discipling than we could do at youth group meetings. The foundational or evangelistic messages the rest of the group needed just weren't enough to challenge them. Since the first year we offered the Intensive Discipleship Course (referred to from here on as IDC), we saw a huge increase in the number of students who developed into leaders of their peers and became bold and dynamic examples of what a Christian student should be. Our goal is to produce disciples who are equipped with the power of God to fulfill His purposes throughout the world.

Who Should Do IDC?

Everybody who is hungry to know God more is invited to do IDC. Although the course is designed for young people age fifteen through college age, even adults (including pastors and youth leaders) who have taken the course say it has done a lot for their walk with the Lord. Setting aside time to focus on spiritual growth will benefit anyone who will stick to it.

HOW IT WORKS

LEARNING GOD'S WAYS

IDC will teach you a lot from God's Word, but it will also show you God's ways. Our goal is for you to really get in touch with God, know His heart for you, and discover His plan for your life. You'll learn *principles* instead of just *facts*. This is how you can apply the Lord's unchanging ways to a rapidly changing world.

"He made known His ways to Moses, His acts to the children of Israel." (Psalm 103:7)

"'For My thoughts are not your thoughts, nor are your ways My ways,' says the LORD. 'For as the heavens are higher than the earth, so are My ways higher than your ways, and My thoughts than your thoughts.'" (Isaiah 55:8–9)

IDC will give you solid teaching, lots of challenges, and fresh insights. To benefit from IDC, here's what you will need:

1. Hunger for an intimate walk with the Lord and a lifestyle that is pleasing to Him.

"Oh, that my ways were directed to keep Your statutes!" (Psalm 119:5)

2. Willingness to come to God's Word with an open heart.

"I will meditate on Your precepts, and contemplate Your ways." (Psalm 119:15)

3. Willingness to change in response to the Holy Spirit's work in your life. This may be repentance, making restitution, restoring broken relationships, taking steps of faith, submitting to a call to ministry, or other types of change.

"I thought about my ways, and turned my feet to Your testimonies." (Psalm 119:59)

THE NEED FOR A MENTOR

The dictionary defines a mentor as a wise and trusted person. One of the major components of IDC is spending time with an older and more spiritually mature person who can help you grow in the Lord. In choosing your mentor, look for someone who has a relationship with the Lord that you admire, a person you could confide in, someone easy to get along with and not too busy to spend an hour or so with you each week. This could be one of your parents or a grandparent, your pastor or youth leader, or someone else in your church whom you respect. If you are a teenager, ask your parents whom they would suggest and don't choose a mentor they do not approve of. We urge you not to try to do IDC by yourself—the accountability to another person will help you stick to the course and process the work the Holy Spirit is doing in your life. Guys need to choose a man, and girls should choose a woman if at all possible, but your parents may approve of someone of the opposite sex. All of us—even adults—need mentors. If you are an adult or a college student, obviously you don't need parental permission in choosing a mentor, but it's wise to choose prayerfully.

When you've found someone you would like to ask to be your mentor, make an appointment to see him or her and show the person your IDC book. Have the potential mentor read the section of this book called "Mentoring an Intensive Discipleship Course Student." You may want to leave the book with the potential mentor for a couple of days so that he or she really understands what IDC is. Make sure the mentor understands the commitment he or she is making to you and has the time to follow through with it. This is especially important with busy church staff members. If the person agrees, fill out the Course Commitment form on pages 25–26, sign it, and have your parents (if you are a teenager) and your mentor sign it.

Each week when you meet with your mentor, you'll show him or her the study you have done and talk about what the Lord is doing in your life. Make a commitment to be open and vulnerable. Since your mentor is a wise and trusted person,

be honest about the victories and the needs in your life. If something comes up partway through IDC and your mentor can't follow through on his or her commitment, you can still complete the course and learn a lot from it. Don't give up!

COURSE REQUIREMENTS

Weekly teachings. This IDC book is about character development. During the twelve-week course, you'll complete one Bible study each week. Don't wait until the last minute, but do a little each day and let the teaching sink in. Each of the twelve teachings focuses on one aspect of what it takes to be useful to God and to reflect His character to the world. We know that a teaching on holiness, humility, or any other character quality is not what changes our lives. Spiritual growth doesn't happen by learning concepts and facts or even by memorizing Bible verses. It is a change of heart that comes as a result of seeing more clearly than ever before who God is and responding to what we see in Him (2 Corinthians 3:18). It is allowing Him to mold us into the image of Jesus (Romans 12:1–2). Because of this, Bible study needs to be followed by prayer about the way the Lord wants to apply the message to our lives. This is crucial. We don't want you to complete twelve weeks of IDC and leave with your head stuffed full of truth but your heart unchanged. Take your time with the teachings. There's no need to rush through them. You'll get a lot more out of IDC if you let God have time to work in your heart.

Whenever you see Scripture references throughout the text, look them up and write them *in your own words* on the lines provided. This will cause you to think through what each verse means and not simply copy a verse that you don't understand. The margins next to the teachings will allow you to write down thoughts and questions and anything the Lord shows you during your times of study.

After each teaching, you'll find a page of questions. The application questions are meant to be answered right away while everything is still fresh in your mind. After you've had a day or two or three to think about the teaching, to digest it a little, go back and answer the follow-up questions. Don't hurry through them—take your time.

Daily Bible reading. IDC concentrates on learning the New Testament first. Many Christian students have never read the entire New Testament, and most have never developed consistent habits of daily Bible reading. By dividing the New Testament into daily, fifteen-minute segments, you can read it in less than three months. If you fall behind schedule, try to catch up as soon as possible, before you get too far behind. With only fifteen minutes per day of reading required, it isn't too hard to get back on schedule. If you have been reading the Old Testament or another part of the New Testament when the course begins, we ask you to put that study on hold for the duration of the course.

Be sure to read a translation of the Bible that you can understand. The New King James Version and the New International Version are highly recommended. Each week you can mark passages that you find confusing and ask questions at the next meeting with your mentor.

Scripture memory. Each week you'll memorize two verses or brief Bible passages. You don't have to get every word exactly; have a clear grasp of the verse and memorize it as closely as you can. We suggest that you write out the verses on a piece of paper or a 3 x 5 card and carry it with you. Read the verses throughout the week. It's not hard to memorize Scripture with enough repetition, but don't just memorize it as a parrot would, getting all the words right but having no idea what it means.

Prayer and fasting. Just as Jesus' disciples asked Him to teach them to pray, we need to learn to have an effective prayer life. The fifteen-minutes-per-morning requirement shown on the course commitment form is only about one percent of our daily lives, and yet many Christians don't spend that much time each day giving God their undivided attention. Once you begin at this level, it won't be long before you're thinking of more things to pray about and spending more time each day with the Lord.

Fasting builds spiritual discipline. You may have never fasted before except between meals, and then only if it was absolutely necessary. Believe it or not, you can actually survive for a day without food! Just look at the people in the Bible who fasted for forty days. Each month you'll pick a day to fast when your schedule isn't packed. Be sure to drink lots of liquids. You'll find that if you start feeling weak and hungry, your strength will come back if you'll pray. I always fast before important spiritual events, such as a youth camp or missions trip, and whenever I'm really burdened with a personal need or a problem in the life of someone I care about. God comes through when we seek Him with our whole hearts! Your mentor will be able to explain more about fasting.

Caution: Not everyone should participate in fasting. People who have health conditions or are taking medication should consult their physician about whether they should fast. All teenage students should discuss fasting with a parent and make sure that that parent is specifically aware of the days of a fast.

Spiritual growth questionnaires. On the first day of the course you will evaluate your spiritual life by filling out the Spiritual Growth Questionnaire 1. On the last day of the course you will fill out the Spiritual Growth Questionnaire 2, again evaluating each area of your spiritual life. You will then be able to compare the two questionnaires so that you can chart your growth in each area.

Missions report. Using *Operation World*, by Patrick Johnstone and Jason Mandryk, or another

Christian missions resource, you will fill out the Missions Report page (during week 2) on a nation that interests you. Pray for the nation regularly, and don't be surprised if a concern for its people grows in your heart to the extent that the Lord calls you to go there to serve Him! This is exactly what happened to me with the nation of India. Beginning in Bible school in the early 1980s, I prayed for India as part of a class assignment, and I've ended up there three times so far, with plans to return.

Your salvation testimony. Spending time to take stock of what the Lord has already done in your life and writing out your testimony will help you be ready to share the gospel whenever the opportunity comes up. Some people who grew up in Christian homes and have served the Lord since their childhood feel that they don't have a testimony. They think that only stories of past evil deeds are interesting to others, but any testimony showing the reality of God in one's life is valid and will speak to those who don't know Him. Unsaved people can argue with doctrine but have a hard time explaining away a story of divine intervention, protection, provision, or especially a living relationship with one's Creator. Your salvation testimony, which you'll write during week 5, should be three to five pages.

Book reports. During IDC you'll be reading two true stories from the following list. You can read other books if you like, but these are some of the best. It's easy for people to let their minds wander during a teaching, but a good story keeps everyone's attention. Lots of students who hate reading have told me that they can't put these books down, and many parents have read the books because their students in IDC had said that the books were so powerful.

- Corrie ten Boom, *The Hiding Place* (Grand Rapids: Chosen Books, 2006).
- Elisabeth Elliot, *Through Gates of Splendor* (Carol Stream, Ill.: Tyndale House, 2005).
- Loren Cunningham, *Is That Really You, God?* (Seattle: YWAM Publishing, 2001).
- Brother Andrew, *God's Smuggler* (Grand Rapids: Chosen Books, 2001).
- Bruce Olson, *Bruchko* (Seattle: YWAM Publishing, 2005).
- Don Richardson, *Lords of the Earth* (Seattle: YWAM Publishing, 2003).
- Don Richardson, *Peace Child* (Seattle: YWAM Publishing, 2003).
- Sister Gulshan Esther, *The Torn Veil* (Grand Rapids: Zondervan, 2004).
- Jackie Pullinger, *Chasing the Dragon* (Ventura, Calif.: Gospel Light, 2004).

The book report forms are included in the appropriate places in the twelve-week course. (Book 1 should be read by week 4, and book 2 should be read by week 9.) The book report is not a time to retell the story. Instead, it is a time to tell what you learned through reading the book and how it affected your relationship with the Lord. The ways God has used the people in the books will amaze you and will challenge you to step out in faith for God to use you as well.

You can order these books through any Christian bookstore. To save money, you may want to see if you can borrow them from your pastor or the church library. After reading them you'll agree that they are so inspiring that you'll want to have your own copies. You will find a list of some of my favorite books at the end of the course. I encourage you to continue reading great Christian books.

You'll notice that most of the books listed above are missionary stories. Every Christian needs to know about missions. Even if you know that God has not called you to go to another country to preach the gospel, He has called you to participate in the Great Commission that Jesus gave to all Christians (Matthew 28:18–20). If you're interested in missions or have heard God's call to the mission field, be sure to read the fascinating book *Operation World*, by Patrick Johnstone and Jason Mandryk. The book covers every country in the world and tells what God is doing there. Spend a little time looking through it and read about countries that interest you—places you'd like to go, the country your ancestors came from, or places you've gone on vacation. Then think about the needs there: What if you lived in China, where Christians are martyred, or Mozambique, where the annual income is eighty dollars? Or Afghanistan, where there are 48,000 Muslim mosques but not one single Christian church? Take time to ask God to bring His kingdom to the ends of the earth. Another great book is *Strongholds of the 10/40 Window*, by George Otis Jr. (YWAM Publishing, 1995). It concentrates on the countries that have the most desperate need for the gospel.

TV and movie reports. Another goal in IDC is for you to examine your TV and movie viewing habits and find out what the Lord thinks about the things you watch. We don't believe that all TV and movies are evil or that it is a sin to watch movies and TV in general. The course commitment doesn't require students to avoid all TV or movies; it only asks students to write a brief report about what they do watch. Just the fact that you are accountable to your mentor and that you'll be writing reports might keep you from watching things you already know in your heart the Lord would not approve. We want you to grow in discernment and not take for granted areas of your life that the Lord may want to change. Many Christians never stop to seek God's will in the areas of entertainment and recreation. You can watch anything you like, but if you do seek God's will about what you watch, you will be viewing it from the Lord's perspective. Then you will let *Him* decide whether it is something you should be spending your time and devotion on. (Please read Changing Your Viewing Habits beginning on this page for further discussion of this course requirement.)

Additional course requirements. In addition to completing the previous course requirements, you are expected to (1) attend church weekly, including Sunday morning services and any youth/college group, (2) spend at least fifteen minutes in prayer every morning, (3) tithe (give 10 percent of all your income to God's work), and (4) allow the Lord complete access to your life.

Course evaluation. Please write us using the course evaluation form at the back of the book and tell us what you thought about IDC. Your opinions will help us improve future editions of the course. Also, we really want to hear how the Lord used IDC in your life.

Changing Your Viewing Habits

Do your viewing habits need to change? Perhaps. If you recognize that sitting in front of a screen and passively absorbing endless hours of the world's values is having a negative effect on your relationship with the Lord, it's time for you to evaluate your habits. When we click through the TV channels or go to the video rental store, we may not find anything that really appeals to us, but we've already planned to set aside time to watch something. We end up watching the least objectionable thing we can find, not necessarily something good. In this way, we squander a great deal of time. Have you ever finished watching a movie and then thought, "That was a total waste of two hours!" In the same way, the addictive nature of playing video games and surfing the Internet makes these activities an incredible time drain.

IDC might help you realize that you've been spending twenty to thirty hours (the U.S. average) in front of a TV or computer or at the theater each week, but you have "never had enough time" to read the Bible. Think of all the other things you could do with the extra time:

- reach out to someone who needs a friend
- improve your grades
- work out
- invest your life in discipling others
- read a good book
- learn the Bible
- start a hobby
- play sports
- pray
- help your mom or dad if you live at home
- get more involved in church

Here are some helpful ways to evaluate TV shows, movies, video games, and Internet browsing:

1. Do you have aftereffects from things you have watched in the past that stir up temptations to sin? We've all had experiences of some recurring thought from the media: a gross or disgusting scene, a fear-producing image, a sensual or explicit picture. Different things will make different people stumble, depending on the weak areas in each person's life. The Lord already knows whether the movie that you'd like to see has elements that will tempt you to sin. Will you ask Him in advance if He wants you to see it? More important, will you obey what He tells you?

2. Have you ever regretted seeing a movie because of these effects? If so, will you ask God to help you stay away from anything that you'll regret later?

3. When we disobey the Lord, we disappoint Him. If God isn't allowing you to see a particular movie or TV show, how much of your fellowship and intimacy with God are you going to lose if you do so anyway? If you're ministering to others, how much of the anointing of God will you give up in exchange for that movie? Of course, we know that God will forgive us if we repent later, but aren't we abusing the grace of God to sin with the plan of asking forgiveness afterward?

4. God intends for us to remain in constant fellowship with Him. Will that movie or TV program cause you to live in a world without God for an hour or two?

5. Does the program ridicule God, people who believe in Him, the authority of parents, and the holiness of sex in marriage? Does it slowly whittle away the foundations of what you believe? Situation comedies are especially guilty of this. They make us take lightly the things God takes seriously. We laugh at evil, and it doesn't seem so evil anymore. Does the movie lie to you about the way God made the universe? Does it deny the law of reaping what we sow or the fact that this life is temporary and eternity never ends?

"Fools mock at sin." (Proverbs 14:9)

"Neither filthiness, nor foolish talking, nor coarse jesting, which are not fitting, but rather giving of thanks." (Ephesians 5:4)

6. Let's not hide behind the deception that since we are so strong in the Lord, the things that cause others to stumble won't affect us. There are some things that God simply doesn't want us to see or hear.

"I will behave wisely in a perfect way. Oh, when will You come to me? I will walk within my house with a perfect heart. I will set nothing wicked before my eyes; I hate the work of those who fall away; it shall not cling to me. A perverse heart shall depart from me; I will not know wickedness." (Psalm 101:2–4)

"Turn away my eyes from looking at worthless things, and revive me in Your way." (Psalm 119:37)

These things that God wants us to avoid include the following:

- Horror movies that glorify evil, exalt the kingdom of darkness, and make God seem either powerless or completely absent. Horror movies are a fantasy about the world the way Satan would like it to be if it weren't for the restraining hand of God.

- Sensual and suggestive comments that create mental images of sexual sin.
- Explicit or implied sexual scenes, which filmmakers design to cause you to identify with one of the people involved. God didn't make that beautiful girl or handsome guy for you to lust over! What you are seeing in a bedroom scene should be reserved for that person's spouse. For anyone else to view him or her in that way is sin.

7. How's the language? We know that God's Name deserves respect. Is the language crude, offensive, disgusting? What does the Lord think about it? Hearing a lot of profanity makes it much easier for those words to come to mind when we stub our toes, drop something that breaks, or get frustrated. Are you conditioning your mind to react with impatience and anger rather than looking to the Lord when things don't go smoothly?

8. The Bible contains lots of violence, but the media have a way of lingering on the gruesome results rather than simply telling the story. Are you watching sensationalized, gory violence? Does it cheapen the value of human life in your eyes? Does it train your mind to think that violence is an appropriate response to others?

9. Will you be courageous enough to be the one among your Christian friends who says no to certain movies, who gets up and walks out of the theater, who insists on changing the channel? This may be costly in terms of your immediate reputation, but it will gain you respect as one who takes following the Lord seriously and will bring conviction to those who aren't listening to their consciences. You see, the Holy Spirit is trying to bring to them the same sense of His disapproval over an ungodly movie.

"You shall not follow a crowd to do evil." (Exodus 23:2)

"The sinners in Zion are afraid; fearfulness has seized the hypocrites: 'Who among us shall dwell with the devouring fire? Who among us shall dwell with everlasting burnings?' He who walks righteously and speaks uprightly…who stops his ears from hearing of bloodshed, and shuts his eyes from seeing evil: he will dwell on high; his place of defense will be the fortress of rocks; bread will be given him, his water will be sure. Your eyes will see the King in His beauty; they will see the land that is very far off." (Isaiah 33:14–17)

NOTE TO PARENTS ABOUT THE COURSE

may or may not choose to ask their parents to be their mentor. Don't feel rejected if your children ask someone else. This is a natural part of the maturing process for a student. Parents can still be involved through prayer and encouragement and by asking questions and reading the book-report books.

Important Note: Please be aware that one of the course commitments is for students to fast one day per month. Some people, because of health conditions or medication, should not participate in fasting. Please discuss fasting with your son or daughter and know specifically when he or she goes on a fast. If you have any questions or concerns about the appropriateness of fasting for your son or daughter, please contact your physician.

IDC is a proven method of spiritual growth. Previous versions of this course have gone across America and to every continent. The course is demanding, but it follows the necessary steps for producing strong disciples. We feel that the church needs to challenge today's youth. The requirements of the course will stretch young people spiritually and teach them responsibility, faithfulness, and ways to set and achieve goals.

We urge parents to be involved in IDC with their sons and daughters. One course requirement is for students to choose a mentor, and students

Mentoring a student

MENTORING AN INTENSIVE DISCIPLESHIP COURSE STUDENT

It is an honor when a young person interested in taking the Intensive Discipleship Course (IDC) chooses you to be his or her mentor. It shows that the person has a great deal of respect for you and sees in you a relationship with the Lord that is worthy of imitation. This intensive, twelve-week course focuses on the personal discipleship that takes place between a student and a mentor. IDC contains a solidly evangelical perspective and focuses on the Lord Jesus Christ and young people's relationship with Him.

IDC is a demanding course, but Christian young people need a radical challenge. Powerful results in the lives of hundreds of students over the past decade show the value of this approach. Any young person who wants to play on a school sports team, perform in a band, or excel in any field must diligently apply effort to the endeavor. Unfortunately, in Christian circles all we usually ask of young people is consistent attendance at our meetings. We, the creators of IDC, believe it is also necessary to call young people to diligence, faithfulness, self-discipline, and responsibility in their relationship with the Lord. We believe as well that young people will rise to the occasion if we encourage and support them.

We urge you to look through this material carefully and be sure that you have the time to fulfill the commitment you are making by agreeing to be a mentor. To disciple a young person in this way will undoubtedly take an effort on your part to free up time in your schedule, but the rewards will definitely be worth it.

YOUR ROLE AS A MENTOR

Your role as a mentor is different from that of a schoolteacher. You won't need to correct papers, read many reports, or give grades. Instead, your primary job will be to be available, to be open and honest with the student about your own walk with God, and to help him or her walk through a process of study and spiritual growth. You'll meet with your student each week for one to two hours.

Each week students work through a teaching designed to challenge and stimulate their walk with Jesus. They read many verses of Scripture, which they write down in their own words. This enables students to grasp the essence of each verse and not simply copy it without understanding its meaning. Students answer questions at the end of each teaching and seek the Lord to apply the teaching to their lives. When you meet with your student, you will ask what he or she studied and discuss how the Lord is dealing with the student in that particular area of life. Reading the study questions at the end of the teaching and the student's answers to the questions will help you see what the Lord is doing in your student's heart.

Each week your student will memorize two Scripture passages and will recite them to you. The student will also turn in two brief book reports during the course. Sometimes the student will have written TV or movie reports, and the student will turn in one salvation testimony for you to read. You can briefly look at the student's Daily Bible Reading chart at the beginning of each teaching to make sure that the student is keeping up with the reading. Daily Bible reading should bring up questions that your student can write down on the chart and ask you to explain. Don't be afraid to say that you don't know the answer: there are plenty of passages in Scripture that mystify all of us. You might suggest other scriptures or recommend Christian books on a particular subject. You may want to present both sides of a controversial topic. Perhaps the best answer to a question you can't answer is, "Let's try to find out together."

Asking your student questions to stimulate his or her seeking the Lord to find the answer is preferable to handing out the answer. In discipling young people, we must be careful to avoid encouraging them to depend on us for answers. Our job as leaders is to be facilitators of learning rather than spiritual gurus. We don't have all the answers, and we must make this clear to the young people while pointing them to the One who does have all the answers. We are to let them find their own revelation from God's Word as we help them know the Holy Spirit as their teacher.

"But the anointing which you have received from Him abides in you, and you do not need that anyone teach you; but as the same anointing teaches you concerning all things, and is true, and is not a lie, and just as it has taught you, you will abide in Him." (1 John 2:27)

"But the Helper, the Holy Spirit, whom the Father will send in My name, He will teach you all things, and bring to your remembrance all things that I said to you." (John 14:26)

You must be willing to help your student wrestle through difficulties and painful but necessary changes without allowing an unhealthy dependency on you. It is frequently the tendency of those with a shepherd's heart to try to make life easy for their flock, sometimes blunting the sharp edges of God's Word in the process. Yet you must allow the Lord to deal with your student and not abort the process of conviction in his or her life.

A mentor's message, though always spoken with compassion and love, must be "Here is truth—what are you and the Lord going to do about it?" Students will respond in one of three ways. The first response is to feel miserable and condemned, which can lead some to hardening their hearts. We must steer them past this obstacle, giving hope that the grace of God will transform them. The second response is to try to improve, which results in legalism, performance orientation, and either spiritual pride or more condemnation. Again, we must steer students toward genuine heart change. The third response is the one we desire—lasting transformation by the work of the Holy Spirit.

You will not need to personally oversee some of the other parts of the student's commitment, such as tithing, church attendance, fasting, or daily prayer. The student is on the honor system for those aspects of the course.

Building a relationship in which your student feels comfortable in sharing personal thoughts, feelings, and needs is essential. Your interest and questions can draw the student into being open with you. Trust and confidentiality are part of the foundation for discipling a young person, who may entrust you with deep hurts, secrets, or confessions of sin. You'll need to use great care and wisdom to decide whether or not to disclose such matters and how to discuss them with the student's parents if you choose to disclose.

Don't be afraid to be honest with the young person you are discipling. If God could use only people who had everything worked out in their lives, I would certainly be disqualified, and probably you would be too! I've found that being vulnerable and open about my weaknesses allows students to feel confident in discussing their struggles. On the other hand, a leader who gives the appearance of having it all together can intimidate young people, causing them to fear being rejected, judged, or condemned if they confess sins or areas of weakness. Let's be careful to create an environment where openness and honesty prevail (Proverbs 28:13).

During the week, we urge you to pray for your student and hear insights from the Lord to bring up the next time you meet with the student. Each week when you meet together, be sure to close in prayer to take before the Lord the specific needs of the student and the area of teaching he or she is studying.

Either you or the student you are discipling may have an extra busy week or have to miss your meeting for another reason, such as vacation, illness, or final exams. As soon as possible, reschedule the meeting so that the student doesn't lose momentum. If the student falls behind and hasn't completed the week's assignments by the day of your meeting, don't cancel the meeting. You can still talk and pray together. Encourage the student to catch up as soon as possible and follow up to see that the student does so. Many students need adult help in carrying through with their commitments.

We suggest a graduation ceremony or celebration of some kind for the student upon completion of the course. Include the parents and friends of the student. Award a diploma to commend the work done by the student. This is a great way to recognize the student publicly when he or she has completed the course. Encourage the student to watch for spiritual pride, and then speak of the student's accomplishments in a way that will encourage others to take bold steps of spiritual growth. This can be a good witness to the church that some students are godly and dedicated to walking with the Lord. It may also be convicting for some of the church members, including other young people.

The Goal of Discipleship: Looking Beyond IDC

The result of the process of discipleship should be that disciples become disciplers. The following scripture outlines three phases in this process.

"For Ezra had prepared his heart to seek the Law of the Lord, and to do it, and to teach statutes and ordinances in Israel." (Ezra 7:10, emphasis added)

The first step is seeking and learning God's ways. Next comes living out what we have learned. Finally, we teach others His ways. The order here is crucial, and all three steps are necessary for discipleship to be complete. Some people try to live the Christian life without a genuine understanding of it and end up inventing their own versions of Christianity. Others try to teach what they haven't worked out in their own lives and sometimes bring reproach on the Lord and the church. Still others seek and do but never teach, and the chain of events from the Patriarchs through the cross and the Church finds a dead end in their lives: they never pass the gospel on to others. As leaders of young people, we need to aim their spiritual lives in such a way that the truth we pass on to them continues to affect the world for generations to come.

"And the things that you have heard from me among many witnesses, commit these to faithful men who will be able to teach others also." (2 Timothy 2:2)

Pastors and Youth Leaders with Multiple Students

One option for a pastor or youth leader is to have several key students take the course at the same time and meet for discipleship and mentoring in a small group. Be sure not to let this group become too large, or the personal nature of it will be lost. We recommend no more than five young people at a time in a small group. If you have many young people you would like to have take the course, either raise up other qualified small-group leaders or teach the course in a large group with smaller discussion groups. Follow the same course guidelines as for mentors with one student.

Student Progress Chart

Here is a chart to help you keep track of your student's progress through the course. Check the appropriate box when the student has completed each assignment.

Week	Scriptures Memorized	Daily Bible Reading	Teaching and Study Questions Completed	Assignments Due
1				Spiritual Growth Questionnaire 1
2				Missions Report
3				
4				Book Report 1
5				Salvation Testimony
6				
7				
8				
9				Book Report 2
10				
11				
12				Spiritual Growth Questionnaire 2 / Course Evaluation

MENTOR'S COURSE EVALUATION

We value your input! When the student has completed the course, please take a few minutes to give us your suggestions and comments.

Mentor's name:

Address:

Phone: E-mail:

Name of student(s):   Age of student(s):

Dates of course:

1. Please rate the following on a scale of 1 to 10, with 10 as the best rating:

• Quality of materials	1	2	3	4	5	6	7	8	9	10
• Ease of use	1	2	3	4	5	6	7	8	9	10
• Practical value of teachings	1	2	3	4	5	6	7	8	9	10
• Effect of the course on the student	1	2	3	4	5	6	7	8	9	10
• Format of the book	1	2	3	4	5	6	7	8	9	10

2. What were the strongest points of the course?

3. What were the weakest points?

4. What, if any, parts of the course did you feel were unnecessary?

5. What, if any, other topics would you like to have seen covered?

6. Other suggestions for improvement?

Thanks for your help!
Please mail to Vinnie Carafano, 936 W. Sunset, El Paso, TX 79922

Course Commitment

Carefully read and fill out this course commitment after discussing the course with your parents (if you are a teenager) and your mentor and receiving their approval to go ahead.

Name: Age:

Address: Phone:

Mentor's name:

Please answer the following three questions on a separate sheet of paper:
1. How did you become a Christian, and how is your relationship with the Lord now?
2. Why do you want to participate in the Intensive Discipleship Course?
3. What are your goals in your relationship with Jesus?

You are about to enter a time of great spiritual growth. This statement of commitment will show your decision to the Lord, your parents, your mentor, and yourself that you have set aside the next three months to focus on seeking God, doing those things that will help you grow in Him, and being accountable to spiritual leadership.

I commit to do the following:
1. Complete all twelve sessions of the course.
2. Read the entire New Testament.
3. Read two of the recommended books and write a one-page report on each book.
4. Attend church weekly—Sunday morning and youth/college group.
5. Memorize twenty-four assigned Scripture verses.
6. Fast one designated day each month.
7. Spend at least fifteen minutes in prayer every morning.
8. Tithe (give 10 percent of all my income to God's work).
9. Allow the Lord complete access to my life.
10. Write out my salvation testimony (3–5 pages).
11. Research and write a one-page missions report on the nation of my choice.

I will be accountable to do the following:
1. Keep up, or improve, the school grades I am earning now.
2. Put ungodly influences out of my life:
   - For the next twelve weeks I will listen only to Christian music.
   - For any movie or TV show I watch (other than the news, sports, or documentaries) I will write a brief summary of the plot and comments on the movie or show from God's perspective.

Continued on next page...

3. Keep Jesus as my first love (Revelation 2:4). This includes putting aside dating relationships and romances for the next twelve weeks and setting the time apart to seek the Lord without being distracted. Parents of a teenager and the mentor can make an exception to this commitment for a student dating another committed Christian before the course begins.

No one will be looking over your shoulder to see whether you are fulfilling these three commitments. Their purpose is to help you grow, and you will benefit from IDC according to the degree you are willing to enter into the spirit of it.

Don't overload your schedule. If you have a difficult semester load of classes or a job and take IDC, you won't be able to do your best in any of these areas. Prayerfully decide whether this is the right time for you to make this commitment and, if so, how you will rearrange your schedule.

Parents' Commitment (for teenagers)

I have read the course requirements and believe that this is a valuable experience for my son or daughter. I will encourage him or her in spiritual growth and pray for him or her daily.

_____

Mentor's Commitment

I have read the course requirements and believe that this is a valuable experience for a Christian young person. I will encourage him or her in spiritual growth, meet each week for twelve weeks, and pray for him or her daily.

_____

Student's Commitment

I have read the course requirements and know that it will be tough, but I'm going to give the course my very best and become a man or woman of God. I'm ready for the challenge!

_____

12 WEEKS OF CHALLENGE

GET READY for a challenging twelve-week adventure with God. In the Intensive Discipleship Course you'll learn more about the Lord and the Bible than ever before. But this course is not for everyone. It's demanding…and it will change your life.

Are you ready to take the challenge?

SCRIPTURE MEMORY

Acts 4:12 Nor is there salvation in any other, for there is no other name under heaven given among men by which we must be saved.

Colossians 2:8–10 Beware lest anyone cheat you through philosophy and empty deceit, according to the tradition of men, according to the basic principles of the world, and not according to Christ. For in Him dwells all the fullness of the Godhead bodily; and you are complete in Him, who is the head of all principality and power.

FILL OUT SPIRITUAL GROWTH QUESTIONNAIRE 1 ON THE NEXT PAGE.

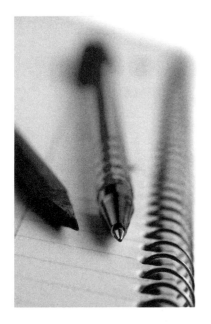

DAILY BIBLE STUDY

✓ Check when completed		
Sunday	Matthew 1–4	_____
Monday	Matthew 5–7	_____
Tuesday	Matthew 8–11	_____
Wednesday	Matthew 12–15	_____
Thursday	Matthew 16–19	_____
Friday	Matthew 20–23	_____
Saturday	Matthew 24–25	_____

BIBLE-READING QUESTIONS

_____
_____
_____
_____
_____
_____
_____
_____
_____
_____

PRAYER NEEDS THIS WEEK

_____
_____
_____
_____
_____
_____
_____
_____
_____
_____
_____
_____

Spiritual Growth Questionnaire 1

1. My relationship with the Lord is

(distant)   1   2   3   4   5   6   7   8   9   10   (intimate)

2. My knowledge of the Bible is

(very little)   1   2   3   4   5   6   7   8   9   10   (very much)

3. My Bible reading is

(inconsistent) 1   2   3   4   5   6   7   8   9   10   (steady)

4. My awareness of missions is

(very little)   1   2   3   4   5   6   7   8   9   10   (very much)

5. My understanding of God's plan for my life is

(very little)   1   2   3   4   5   6   7   8   9   10   (very much)

6. My prayer life is

(nonexistent) 1   2   3   4   5   6   7   8   9   10   (powerful)

ADDITIONAL COMMENTS FOR YOURSELF (OPTIONAL):

_____

_____

_____

_____

_____

_____

_____

_____

Lesson one

Practical Keys to Learning God's Word

Many Christians are ashamed of their ignorance of God's Word. They become discouraged when they can't find the verses they look for. *Hmm,* they wonder, *wasn't it on the left side of the page about halfway down?* Because of this unfamiliarity with God's Word, they are afraid to witness. After all, what if the person they are witnessing to spouts, "So the Bible says that, huh? Show me!"

Because all they know of God comes secondhand from others, these believers are jealous of those who know the Bible well. Like a baby bird with its mouth open, they eagerly await spiritual food from someone who has put in the time and effort to learn God's Word. The Lord calls us as Christians to know and live out His Word. "All Scripture is given by inspiration of God, and is profitable for doctrine, for reproof, for correction, for instruction in righteousness, that the man of God may be complete, thoroughly equipped for every good work" (2 Timothy 3:16–17).

God calls all people to know His Word. He used ordinary men like shepherds and fishermen to write His Word (see Acts 4:13). Although the Bible's message is so rich that we'll never discover all that's in it (see Romans 11:33), the truth of the Bible is simple enough for a child to understand (see 2 Timothy 3:15). The big question is, Will we discipline ourselves to learn it?

With a little discipline we can learn the Bible. An average reader spending only fifteen minutes each day can read the whole Bible in less than one year. The New Testament takes less than three months to read, and you will read all of it during this course. Instead of looking at how thick your Bible is and feeling that it's hopeless to expect that you'll ever know God's Word, realize that by breaking it into smaller parts, you can accomplish your goal. Once you complete it, you'll have a sense of achievement. "A desire accomplished is sweet to the soul" (Proverbs 13:19).

The Word of God

The Bible is not a book we can learn on our own by using our minds alone or relying on the wisdom of others. God's Word is different from all other books. (Write out the following and all subsequent verses *in your own words.*)

John 6:63

_____

_____

1 Corinthians 2:12–14

_____

_____

_____

Because the Bible is a spiritual book, we can fully understand it only with the help of our Teacher, the Holy Spirit, who dwells inside us and brings truth into our lives.

1 John 2:27

_____

_____

John 14:17

_____

_____

John 16:13

_____

_____

Whenever we hear an anointed pastor or preacher speaking from the Bible, it is the Holy Spirit working through him or her to teach us. Each time you read your Bible, ask the Holy Spirit to show you something new. In this way alone can we come to know God's Word. Without the work of the Holy Spirit, we have no hope of understanding.

PRACTICAL STRATEGIES

Reading the Bible doesn't have to be a difficult task. Here are some practical suggestions for getting the most out of studying the Bible. Keep them in mind as you work through this course, and if a strategy isn't working for you, try something different.

Use a translation of the Bible that you can understand. Since old-fashioned language can be a barrier to your learning, choose a more modern Bible translation. The New King James Version (NKJV) and the New International Version (NIV) are both good, readable versions. Some other easy-to-read translations, however, sacrifice accuracy for the sake of clarity. Christians who are committed to the study of God's Word may want to avoid these versions.

Make Bible reading a daily habit. It's easy to let days at a time slip by without reading God's Word. For this reason, set aside a specific time in your daily schedule for the Bible, preferably in the morning before your day gets busy. Avoid leaving your reading until late at night, when you're likely to fall asleep. The Word of God is something to be treasured.

Job 23:12

_____

_____

A well-known missionary took Job 23:12 very seriously and made a rule to discipline himself. Since he had a hard time making time for daily readings, his motto was "No Bible, no breakfast." In other words, he wouldn't eat each day unless he had read his Bible first. This strategy would definitely motivate most people to read the Bible.

Set a goal and a time limit. During this course, your goal is to read the New Testament in eleven weeks. The course lasts twelve weeks, which will give those who get behind schedule a chance to catch up and others time to begin rereading the New Testament or start reading the Old Testament.

Goals must be reasonable and measurable. A reasonable goal is something that you can actually expect to accomplish. "I'm going to read the Old Testament this weekend" is not reasonable. A goal must be measurable so that you can know when you've accomplished it. "I'm going to learn the Bible better" is not very measurable. Here are some examples of reasonable, measurable goals you can set when you have completed this course and need a new goal: read the Old Testament in nine months, read Proverbs in one month, read Psalms in two months. It's a great feeling to accomplish such goals and learn God's Word.

Always keep a pen, pencil, or highlighter handy when you read the Bible. Most of what God will ever need to say to you can be found within the covers of the Bible, and you will want to keep track of what the Holy Spirit shows you. Don't be afraid to underline, highlight, or insert brackets around meaningful passages or to write notes in the margin. Write down what the Lord says to you as well as references to other verses on the same topics. If your Bible has a reference system, look up the passage or passages that relate to a verse you find interesting. Also, whenever you hear a verse in a sermon or read one in a Christian book and it seems to speak to you, mark it so that you can find it later.

When you finish reading a book of the Bible, go back through it and review the marked passages and the notes you have made. Then go over it again, and then again. In this way, you'll fix the contents of each book of the Bible in your memory. Having verses marked in your Bible can also help you in witnessing to others. You may want to find some good gospel tracts and mark the verses they quote so that you can find them quickly.

Mark the date you begin and end reading a book of the Bible at the end of that book. By doing this, you'll have a record of how many times you've read a book and how long it has been since you've read that book. When you complete a section of the Bible and want to start another, you can check the dates to see which parts

TRUE STORY

As a zealous, seventeen-year-old, new believer, I shared the gospel with all my friends. One night my best friend Rick asked Jesus into his life. Immediately he said, "My dad needs to hear about this." We went straight to his house, and with high expectations, I told his father how to meet the Lord. You can imagine my shock when Rick's father said, "I've read the Bible cover to cover, and I don't believe it." Every day I was learning so much about the Lord. Scripture had become so real. How could Rick's dad have read more of the Bible than I had and still not believe?

"For indeed the gospel was preached to us as well as to them; but the word which they heard did not profit them, not being mixed with faith in those who heard it." (Hebrews 4:2)

That night I learned that we must respond to Scripture with faith for it to work in our lives. A heart that refuses to believe the revelation of God that the Bible brings will remain in spiritual darkness.

TRUE STORY

The campus men's Bible study was small, but every Tuesday it fed my hunger for God's Word. One day our leader announced that he had to stop leading the group and suggested that one of us take over leadership. The other guys had known the Lord much longer than I had, but none of them would step forward. I volunteered, and they agreed to my offer. But this responsibility was way over my head, and I knew it. I decided to catch up with the others in Bible knowledge and committed to reading ten chapters each day until I had finished the entire Bible.

About three months later, my Bible was brimming with notes and topical lists I had written while reading from Genesis to Revelation. The others in the group were patient as I learned how to communicate the truths of Scripture. We invited campus women to join the group, and the campus ministry grew rapidly. That was in 1978. I've been studying and teaching ever since.

"Your words were found, and I ate them,
And Your word was to me the joy and rejoicing of my
*   heart;*
For I am called by Your name,
O Lord God of hosts." (Jeremiah 15:16)

You, too, can know the Bible thoroughly if you'll put in the hours of work, prayer, and study that it takes to understand God's Word. The payoff is eternal, both for your own relationship with the Lord and for the countless lives you can affect.

of the Bible are fresh in your memory and which aren't. Then you can read the parts that are least fresh in your mind. It is a good idea to read the Bible in blocks: the Gospels, the Epistles, the Minor Prophets, the historical books, the Major Prophets, etc. Many people jump randomly from book to book in their Bible reading but miss the continuity and context of reading Scripture in blocks. The Bible will make more sense to you when read in blocks.

Buy a set of CDs of the Bible and listen to them for forty-five minutes each day. By doing this, you can listen to the New Testament in only three weeks, and the entire Bible takes just three months. Most people can find forty-five minutes a day to listen to CDs—while getting ready for work or school, while driving, etc. This is a useful way to supplement your Bible reading, although nothing replaces time spent reading and studying the Bible and communing with the Holy Spirit.

Buy a concordance or topical Bible to do further study. A biblical concordance is an index of words used in the Bible that provides the words' meanings and locations in the Bible. Concordances and topical Bibles are helpful tools for studying the Bible. Be sure to get a concordance that matches the version of the Bible you use.

MEMORIZING SCRIPTURE

Memorizing Scripture has powerful effects. God's Word can and should be an integral part of your life, protecting and guiding you.

Psalm 119:9–11

_____

_____

When Satan tempted Jesus in the wilderness, Jesus resisted the devil by quoting Scripture. We, too, can use memorized Bible verses to combat temptation. Read the story of Jesus in the wilderness in Matthew 4:1–11 and summarize the importance of it below.

_____

_____

_____

When we memorize Scripture, we are preparing for future circumstances when we will need to use God's Word in sharing our faith, counseling a friend, comforting a hurting person, or dealing with trials in our own lives. Have you ever had the experience of the Holy Spirit bringing just the right verse to mind at just the right time? Jesus said that the Holy Spirit would remind us of all He has said to us.

John 14:26

_____

_____

Many Christians don't think that they can memorize Scripture. Different methods can be used, but repetition is the key. Think about the song lyrics you know. How did you learn them? Probably not by sitting down with the CD and forcing yourself to learn the lyrics. You learned the words by hearing them repeatedly. If you are hungry for God's Word and spend time reading it, you can remember many verses without even trying to memorize them. For verses that are especially significant to your walk with the Lord right now, however, it is well worth your time to use repetition to memorize. Write the verses repeatedly until they come naturally. Make a note card with the verses you are memorizing and carry it with you wherever you go. All of us have spare moments throughout the day that we can use to memorize Scripture.

God promises a blessing to all who humbly take His Word to heart. "'Heaven is My throne, and earth is My footstool…. For all those things My hand has made, and all those things exist,' says the LORD. 'But on this one will I look: On him who is poor and of a contrite spirit, and who trembles at My word'" (Isaiah 66:1–2). Let's learn God's Word!

Application

1. How consistent has your Bible reading been before starting this course?

2. Have you ever set reasonable, measurable goals for your Bible reading? If so, have you achieved them?

3. Which of the practical strategies discussed in this teaching have you used? Which would help your Bible study the most?

4. Have you ever memorized Scripture? If so, was it easy or difficult? Did you use any of the strategies in this teaching?

Follow-Up

1. How has your Bible reading been this week?

2. List two things you learned from your Bible reading this week.

3. Did you discover anything new in Scripture passages that you have read many times before?

4. Has the Holy Spirit brought Scripture to your mind this week? When and how?

SCRIPTURE MEMORY

James 5:16 Confess your trespasses to one another, and pray for one another, that you may be healed. The effective, fervent prayer of a righteous man avails much.

1 John 3:21–22 Beloved, if our heart does not condemn us, we have confidence toward God. And whatever we ask we receive from Him, because we keep His commandments and do those things that are pleasing in His sight.

COMPLETE THE MISSIONS REPORT ON THE NEXT PAGE.

DAILY BIBLE STUDY

✓ Check when completed

Sunday	Matthew 26–28	_____
Monday	Mark 1–3	_____
Tuesday	Mark 4–7	_____
Wednesday	Mark 8–10	_____
Thursday	Mark 11–13	_____
Friday	Mark 14–16	_____
Saturday	Luke 1–2	_____

BIBLE-READING QUESTIONS

_____
_____
_____
_____
_____
_____
_____
_____

PRAYER NEEDS THIS WEEK

_____
_____
_____
_____
_____
_____
_____
_____
_____

2

Missions Report

We recommend using *Operation World* (21st Century Edition), by Patrick Johnstone and Jason Mandryk, as a reference.

Country name:

Capital:

Population:

Ethnic groups:

Official language(s):

Literacy rate:

Average income (or GDP per capita):

Major religions:

Percentage of evangelical Christians:

Number of missionaries to the country:

Prayer needs:

  1.

  2.

  3.

  4.

Developing Your Prayer Life, Part 1: Intimacy with God

Almost everyone prays. Even atheists have been known to turn toward heaven when problems overwhelm them (Psalm 50:15), and despite the Supreme Court, kids still pray in school when they take tests. Christians pray more frequently than others do, but few Christians have developed a strong prayer life. By this we mean more than the usual sort of prayer: before meals, when we need something, when we're in trouble, or before we fall asleep at night. A strong prayer life involves more than just regular devotions that limit our time with God to fifteen or thirty or sixty minutes each morning. Have you desired closer communication with the Lord? Here are some answers. During the next two weeks, we'll be talking about two important aspects of your prayer life: intimacy with God and spiritual warfare.

God's Desire for Intimacy with Us

God wants to know you. He created the first man and woman because He desired to have a relationship with someone. He walked with Adam through the Garden of Eden, a perfect paradise where there was no sin or suffering, until Adam lost that privilege (Genesis 3:23–24) through sin, breaking the one commandment that God had given him (Genesis 2:16–17). The same God who put an angelic guard to keep disobedient Adam out of the garden later tore the veil in the Jewish temple that symbolically separated humankind from God (Matthew 27:51), showing that through Jesus we could again have fellowship with Him.

To understand the Lord's desire to be intimately involved in our lives, we need to understand why He created us. He didn't want humankind just to be like pets and entertain Him, or He would have stopped on the fifth day of creation. He didn't want us just to be servants—He already has countless angels who could do a much better job than we do. He wanted friends—sons and daughters who would choose to know and love Him. The Father wants us to have the same kind of relationship with Him that Jesus has, and Jesus has called us into a special friendship with Him.

John 1:12

_____

_____

John 15:15

_____

_____

2 Corinthians 6:16–7:1

_____

_____

_____

God offers to dwell with us, but we usually only visit with Him. He offers us fellowship and friendship, but we settle for formality. He wants a relationship with us, but instead we are religious. He calls us to come close, but we are businesslike with Him.

Have you ever thought about what God does all day? We know what we do: eat, sleep, drive, attend school, and work. God doesn't do any of those things. Keeping the planets spinning doesn't require much effort for the Lord. He isn't busy taking care of problems in the Middle East or natural disasters. He's not preoccupied with people whose problems are more serious than ours are. The medical profession uses a process called triage: the injured with the most pressing needs receive immediate care while the others wait until later. God never does spiritual triage with us! We always have His full attention, and He's big enough to pay full attention to all six billion people on earth at the same time.

As the Lord watches the six billion of us, most people are doing things that dishonor Him: breaking every commandment, hurting each other, worshiping false gods, and rejecting the divine call to come to Jesus. The small fraction of humankind who have a living relationship with the Living God usually live separately from Him through most of their daily lives.

Scripture calls God the Watcher of men (Job 7:20). God is the Shepherd taking care of His sheep (John 10:1–4, 11–16). Sheep aren't very bright animals. They require constant attention or they'll get lost, eat poisonous weeds, or be eaten by wolves. We're not so different! God is watching over us day and night (Psalm 121:3–4).

Steps to Intimacy with God

As our Heavenly Father, God is interested in everything that goes on in our lives. He wants to be involved in all we do, not just during church services and Bible studies. He wants to show His protection, His provision, His wisdom, and His actual Presence in our daily lives. However, so often we box Him into certain parts of our lives and leave Him out of other parts.

Frequently we go through an average day with little contact with the Lord. One way we can see whether or not this is true of us is to think of how often we pray catch-up prayers. Catch-up prayers have nothing to do with the red stuff you pour on a hamburger. They are those prayers that we pray before falling asleep at night to catch up on our day and to talk to God about it. "Dear Lord, thank You for today…This morning I…and then this afternoon…and oh yeah, tonight I…well, good night, Lord. In Jesus' name, amen."

When we find ourselves trying to catch up in prayer, it shows that we haven't involved the Lord in our lives throughout the day. God has watched from a distance because we haven't learned to welcome His Presence and include Him in our daily activities. We have missed a blessing, and He has missed seeing His purpose for creating us fulfilled. Do you forget the Lord throughout the day?

Jeremiah 2:32

_____

_____

The opposite of a catch-up prayer life is being in fellowship with God throughout the day. Our channel of communication with Him is prayer, and Scripture tells us to pray constantly (1 Thessalonians 5:17). Obviously, this can't mean formal, on-our-knees, eyes-closed prayer all day and night, or we'd never get anything else done. God knows that we need to eat, sleep, work, go to school, and have time for recreation. But He wants us to walk in the Spirit, that is, to make a conscious choice to live according to our spiritual nature as a Christian rather than to live separately from God, following the sinful desires and temptations of the world and man's fallen nature. Let's look at this in more detail.

Galatians 5:16–18

_____

_____

_____

_____

The first step in walking in the Spirit is simple obedience. This is the foundation of having a loving relationship with God.

John 14:23

_____

_____

_____

John 15:10

_____

_____

_____

The basis of having an intimate relationship with God is the attitude of our hearts toward Him. Could you picture Jesus rejecting the Father's will or rebelling against Him? No way! It's the same for us. Is there a sin in your life that keeps you from being near the heart of God? If so, is it really worth it to miss experiencing the greatest love in the universe and to sadden the heart of the One who loves you so much? Our response to God's love is love for and faith in Him.

John 16:27

_____

_____

_____

The next step is more than just not walking in the flesh or refusing to give in to temptation and sin. It is consciously choosing to seek God and His will for our lives, to put His priorities ahead of our own, to keep the lines of communication with Him open at all times. We will find that the Holy Spirit will bring to mind Scripture

TRUE STORY

In the early 1980s God began to pursue a relationship with me. I had known the Lord for five years but had never experienced intimate fellowship with Him. At the time, I was a teacher in a Christian school. While grading English papers or answering history questions, I would feel the strangest sensation that the Lord was near. Since I wasn't in the midst of a "spiritual" activity such as prayer or worship, I was puzzled. Throughout the day, the Lord would remind me of His presence in my life and call my attention to Him. I waited for some great revelation or startling insight into truth, but He didn't seem to be saying anything. This sensation was not just a feeling —it was more like the spiritual equivalent of a tap on the shoulder. It was an awareness of the reality of God's desire to be involved in my life. At first, I didn't know how to respond to it; then I began to understand, and I talked with Him about even the little, ordinary things in life. I learned how to see things from His perspective and how to walk with Him. God will be tapping on *your* shoulder. Will you respond to Him?

that we can meditate on and that applies to situations we find ourselves in. We then can talk to the Lord all day long, and He talks to us, not necessarily in an audible voice, but communicating His heart and feelings to us. We instantly sense His approval or disapproval of what we say and do and think. It's as though there is a divine thumbs-up or thumbs-down toward our conduct, and we learn to pay attention to His approval or disapproval of things we are thinking about saying or doing before actually saying or doing them. This is very different from the common experience of taking action, then discovering that we did the wrong thing and offended someone else or caused a problem. When we listen to the Lord before rather than after the fact, we can avoid a lot of trouble.

THREE LEVELS OF THE CHRISTIAN'S PRAYER LIFE

Let's illustrate different levels of prayer by three charts. The first level is the usual Christian prayer life—occasional contact with God but long periods spent apart from Him. The person at this level of prayer lives on earth as we all do but rarely makes contact with heaven during the day. This Christian's life is mostly lived independently from God. You may have heard this very wise saying: the more independent you are, the less you pray; the less independent you are, the more you pray. The Lord wants us to realize our need for Him throughout the day.

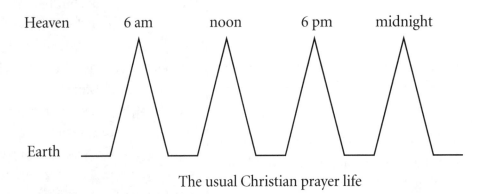

The usual Christian prayer life

The second level is what we would usually think is a strong prayer life—spending time in God's presence at the beginning of each day and praying frequently throughout the day. This person takes time out from earthly life to talk to God more often than does the person at the first level. This level of prayer is an improvement over the first level but still misses God's best. A person can be very religious and do all this but still not have intimate fellowship with God.

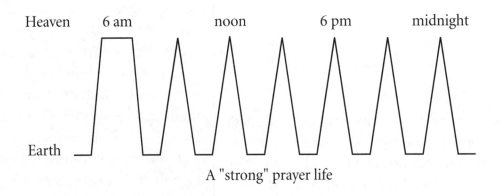

A "strong" prayer life

Here's what God wants to bring us into—waking up each morning with a conscious choice to live in the Spirit and have fellowship with God all day long. This proceeds through a devotional time, but it doesn't end there. Though we go through the usual routines of life, our fellowship with God is unbroken. Mentally and physically we may be fully involved in an earthly task, but spiritually we are alert to and in tune with God. We'll find that a new realization of His Presence lifts our thoughts to Him throughout the day, and our response will be praise, worship, and thanksgiving.

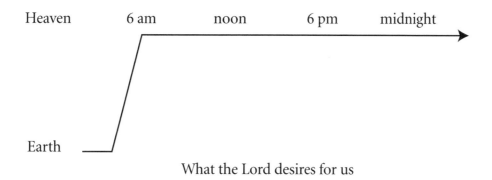

What the Lord desires for us

Throughout our waking hours, we keep the lines of communication with the Lord open, and while we sleep, He can still speak to us. Our spirits are awake, accustomed to being sensitive to the voice of the Lord. Scripture compares our relationship with God and our yearning for God's voice to a couple in love who are eager to hear from each other and often wait excitedly for the beloved to call.

Song of Solomon 5:2

_____

_____

We can cultivate the spiritual sensitivity needed to hear God's voice. The best, though perhaps not so appealing, illustration of this is to compare humans with dogs. Consider something we've all seen: A dog may be sleeping, eating, or walking, but suddenly his ears stand up. Every muscle is tense, and his nose quivers as something that we don't hear captivates him. He is hearing something no one else is hearing. He's ready to take action on it. This needs to be our spiritual posture before the Lord—tuned in to what others miss because the world has clogged up their lives, seeking the voice of God in the midst of ordinary life, and ready to take immediate action. In this kind of life, we will see the Lord's miraculous intervention in our daily circumstances. We will hear and act on divine wisdom, avoid problems and danger, find His provision for our needs, and have answers for the questions and needs of those around us.

Our Response to God's Call to Intimacy

How can you develop this sort of intimacy with God? First, recognize the current level of your fellowship with Him. When you need to pray, how easy is it for you to shift gears? How far are you from walking in the Spirit? When God wants to speak to you, is it local or long-distance? Are you making the daily decision to walk closely with the Lord?

Next, believe the promises of Scripture that the Lord really does want to have fellowship with you despite areas of sin and weakness in your life. Don't wait for feelings of His Presence: receive by faith

God's promises of cleansing and accepting us through the Lord Jesus (Colossians 1:13–14). Too often we think of prayer as a phone call—we spend all our time either dialing (trying to make ourselves good enough to get through to God) or believing that the phone is ringing but He's not answering. By faith we always have access to God. We can talk to Him right now as though He's listening, because He *is* listening. Unless we are intentionally harboring sin in our lives, we can be confident that the Lord will always hear our prayers.

Psalm 66:18

_____

_____

Ephesians 3:12

_____

_____

Hebrews 4:14–16

_____

_____

_____

Hebrews 10:19–22

_____

_____

_____

We can waste a great deal of prayer time trying to feel God's presence. If God met us on the feeling level, we would never grow in faith. Sometimes He withholds feelings to teach us to depend on His Word. We must never try to imagine His presence or work up an experience with God. Faith is a much deeper level of living.

Finally, take every opportunity the Lord gives you to know Him better. When He extends grace to you, never turn Him away. The Holy Spirit has feelings and can be grieved not only by outright sin but also by our disinterest. If our priorities are right we'll never be too busy to have a closer fellowship with God.

Ephesians 4:30

_____

_____

APPLICATION

1. Are you experiencing the intimate fellowship with God that He would like to have with you?

2. Which of the three charts most closely describes your prayer life over the past year?

3. Which chart shows how you would like your prayer life to be?

4. How will you get there?

FOLLOW-UP

1. Has the Lord met with you during any of your prayer times this week?

2. Have you sensed His desire to be involved in your daily life?

3. If so, how?

4. How have you responded to Him?

SCRIPTURE MEMORY

Ephesians 6:13–18 Therefore take up the whole armor of God, that you may be able to withstand in the evil day, and having done all, to stand. Stand therefore, having girded your waist with truth, having put on the breastplate of righteousness, and having shod your feet with the preparation of the gospel of peace; above all, taking the shield of faith with which you will be able to quench all the fiery darts of the wicked one. And take the helmet of salvation, and the sword of the Spirit, which is the word of God; praying always with all prayer and supplication in the Spirit, being watchful to this end with all perseverance and supplication for all the saints.

DAILY BIBLE STUDY

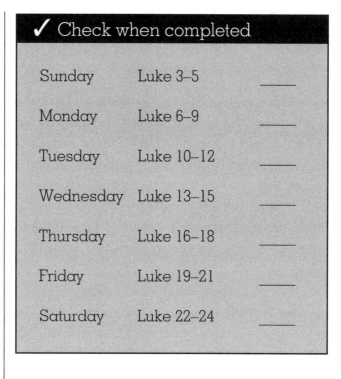

✓ Check when completed

Sunday	Luke 3–5	_____
Monday	Luke 6–9	_____
Tuesday	Luke 10–12	_____
Wednesday	Luke 13–15	_____
Thursday	Luke 16–18	_____
Friday	Luke 19–21	_____
Saturday	Luke 22–24	_____

BIBLE-READING QUESTIONS

_____
_____
_____
_____
_____
_____
_____
_____

PRAYER NEEDS THIS WEEK

_____
_____
_____
_____
_____
_____
_____
_____
_____

3

Lesson three

DEVELOPING YOUR PRAYER LIFE, PART 2: PRAYER AND WARFARE

The previous teaching emphasized the foundational aspect of our prayer lives—our own personal relationship with the Lord. This week's teaching focuses on the next step, an emphasis on praying for the needs of others. The Lord's top priority for our lives is our having an intimate relationship with Him. The second priority is the work that we do for God (Mark 3:14), which includes prayer. When we reverse these two, we end up with religious good deeds instead of a fruitful Christian life. We will become frustrated and dry, wondering why things aren't working out. The natural response is to try harder to produce spiritual results, which is impossible for us if we're living independently from the Lord (John 3:6). Before you try to do any work for the Lord, be sure you're living in a genuine relationship with Him.

PRAYER AS WORK AND BATTLE

A strong prayer life involves real spiritual work and spiritual warfare. Scripture tells of early leaders who labored fervently in prayer (Colossians 4:12), and history shows that the foundation of prayer always comes before the advance of God's kingdom into new areas. Prayer is a direct challenge to Satan's grasp on humankind.

1 John 5:19

_____

_____

We will face spiritual opposition from Satan when we pray. Refer to the charts in the previous teaching that show three levels of a Christian's prayer life. Richard Sibbes, who lived nearly four hundred years ago, said, "When we go to God by prayer, the devil knows we go to fetch strength against him, and therefore he opposeth us all he can." This is still true today. However, the devil doesn't bother trying to interfere with the first level. When was the last time you had a great spiritual battle over saying grace before a meal? The devil gets concerned when we begin a committed devotional life, because that is the first step toward intimacy with God, and intimacy brings power.

Many distractions will come your way to keep you from regular times with God. Still, you're not much of a threat to the kingdom of darkness until you move forward and break through a barrier in your walk with God: the point at which your own life, needs, concerns, and desires no longer are the major motivations in your life. When your focus turns to the purpose of God for your life and to seeing His kingdom come, the battle begins.

One way to gauge the depth of your prayer life is to see how much of your praying revolves around yourself. God knows your needs and has promised to meet them.

Matthew 6:32

_____

_____

Philippians 4:19

_____

_____

Philippians 4:6

_____

_____

_____

We are encouraged to bring our needs before the Lord in prayer, but that is all that many Christians pray about. There's so much more! When we stop being self-centered in prayer and seek His kingdom, which is the loving rule of Jesus over the world, everything else falls into place.

Matthew 6:33

_____

_____

_____

Colossians 3:1–3

_____

_____

_____

_____

We no longer need to spend the majority of our prayer time on selfish topics, and we can devote that time to intercession and prayer for the kingdom to come into the lives of other people. The dictionary defines intercession as "entreaty in favor of another, especially a prayer or petition to God in behalf of another." Satan knows how dangerous this would be to his destructive plans for the world and frequently will stir up lots of personal problems to get our focus back on ourselves. These may include problems in the family, attacks on our health, unexplained discouragement or depression, financial setbacks, school or work troubles, relation-

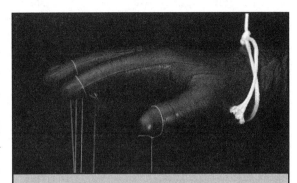

TRUE STORY

During my fourteen years as a youth pastor, one of my highest priorities was campus ministry. Every Tuesday and Thursday for more than a decade I visited two local campuses. Once I was in the cafeteria of one of the toughest high schools in our city. About five hundred students were eating lunch, talking, and laughing when the Lord gave me a startling insight into the spiritual dimension. I saw the kids as marionettes, guided by strings attached to them. The students thought that they were running their own lives, but really they were controlled by the devil through their sins. Some were in bondage to drugs, witchcraft, rebellion, or gangs, but everyone who was unsaved, regardless of his or her bondage, was a captive of the enemy. I realized the need for serious, committed prayer for these students. Our prayers can cut the strings that hold friends, family, fellow students, or even nations in bondage.

ship issues, and a general sense of things going wrong all over the place. By pressing on and walking by faith, keeping our priorities in order, we'll see these attacks subside and victories gained in the lives of those around us. Once we have recognized the source of the problems and have committed ourselves to pursuing God, we can establish a habit of prayer in our lives that takes these obstacles in stride and keeps us moving forward.

The enemy has a strategy in his attack on a serious prayer life. Since he cannot stop prayer from reaching God, his first aim is to stop prayer before it even happens. (His second aim is to keep us from receiving God's answers to our prayers, discussed later in this teaching.) Stopping prayer is Satan's major defense against the power of our prayers, and Satan has an ally that follows us all the way into the prayer closet: our flesh. The flesh doesn't like to pray, fast, or obey God. It is lazy, stubborn, and rebellious. It consistently leans toward selfishness and every kind of sin. That is why God calls us to walk in the Spirit and not in the flesh.

Galatians 5:16–18

_____

_____

_____

Romans 8:6–7

_____

_____

_____

The flesh thrives on feelings and gets discouraged easily. It tells us we have better things to do than pray. The flesh says "Amen" to every argument Satan throws at us to keep us from prayer. Yet no man or woman ever rises above his or her prayer life. We can't grow in intimacy with God if we don't spend time with Him, and we won't see answers to prayers we don't pray. Our effectiveness as Christians begins with our personal fellowship with God. We must not let the flesh defeat us: we must develop a real life of prayer.

HINDRANCES TO PRAYER

We can judge the effectiveness of our prayer life by the opposition of the flesh and the enemy against it. There are many hindrances to prayer, but God has a solution for each one.

Making time for prayer. The greatest hindrance to prayer is making time to do it. Everyone seems to be too busy. The real question is one of priorities—how important is it to you to spend time seeking the Lord, interceding for the needs of family and friends, lifting up a lost world before God's throne? If you are too busy to pray, your life is out of order. What lower priorities have taken over your time and choked out prayer? If necessary, would you take the biblical meaning of _watch_ literally and go without sleep to make time to pray?

Matthew 26:40–41

_____

_____

_____

1 Peter 4:7

_____

Sleepiness. You may find that you're completely awake until you go to pray, and then you immediately become drowsy. This is a spiritual battle—don't give up and take a nap. Also, be aware that you can't pray early in the morning or late at night while nestled all snug in your bed. Even while kneeling in a quiet room you could easily fall asleep, but you'll never fall asleep while walking. Also try praying out loud to keep your mind alert. Realize that late nights kill morning prayer times. If it's really a priority to you to have a powerful time with God in the morning, go to bed early.

Wandering thoughts. Bring every thought into captivity to Christ. Thoughts of pressing needs, an empty stomach, forgotten chores, something we saw on TV, and countless other trains of thought can be distracting. Ask the Lord to rule over your thoughts while you pray to keep you on track. If God reminds you of something you need to do, write it down and keep praying. This is very different from the common experience of having an unfocused mind that goes off on a tangent and then realizing ten minutes later that you're missing your prayer time.

2 Corinthians 10:4–5

When you discover that your mind has wandered, immediately get back to

TRUE STORY

When I was twenty-seven years old, my health crashed. Then my father died suddenly, and grief added to the unusual symptoms I was already experiencing. Several specialists ran tests that showed more things wrong, and they told me they didn't know when I would recover. With two toddlers and a pregnant wife, this was a bad time to be seriously ill. Some days I would lie in bed wide awake but lack the strength to keep my eyes open. After a few months of misery and lots of seemingly unanswered prayer, and with a collapsing ministry and lots of bills, I was very discouraged.

One night we took our young son to see a children's evangelist, who gave an illustration that changed my life. The man used a rope to lasso a folding chair and said that the rope was like faith, while the chair symbolized what we are asking God to do. We can't see whether our faith has really attached itself to the result, but we need to keep praying and pull in the rope to get what we need.

Faith to get well rose up in my heart. I was taking twenty-one prescription pills each day to treat my conditions, and I decided to cut back to twenty. Pain and symptoms flared up. I kept praying and held on by faith and soon felt better, so I cut back to nineteen. Pain rose again, but after a short time I went to eighteen and eventually all the way down to none. This whole process took months, but my health has been great for nearly twenty years. I have learned not to give up and to keep praying.

TRUE STORY

When I first understood the truths depicted in this and the previous teaching on prayer, I decided to set the alarm fifteen minutes earlier than usual so that I'd have time to pray. Several times I heard the Lord tell me that I wouldn't get to where I wanted to be in Him with my current prayer life. I increased my prayer time to thirty minutes, then to one hour each day. I kept hearing the same call to pray more and went to two hours each day. As a full-time youth pastor with the freedom to set my own schedule, I made prayer a priority because of a sense that the Lord had called me as an intercessor. Still hearing a call to intercede more for the youth of our city, I added a three-hour shift every Monday morning. Each week I fasted for one day, and sometimes I fasted for three days, because Jesus said to add fasting to prayer (Matthew 6:16–18). I kept to this timetable for about twelve years. Don't try to copy this schedule, but do what the Lord is calling you to do at each phase of growth in your own prayer life. The perspective on prayer that you've been studying is time-tested and proven by the years that the Lord called me to "labor in prayer," and it will work for you, too.

praying. Just start up where you left off. Don't blow the rest of your prayer time by feeling condemned or guilty. Again, praying out loud helps.

Guilt. All of us have let the Lord down countless times. A feeling of condemnation destroys our confidence toward God, but a stand of faith tells us that God has forgiven and forgotten every sin that we have confessed and forsaken. The blood of the Lamb makes us righteous, and by keeping this in mind, we'll find that our prayers will have powerful effects.

1 John 3:21–22

_____

Proverbs 28:13

_____

1 John 1:8–9

_____

Sometimes guilt is genuine, not an attack of the enemy. (Keep in mind that there is a difference between feeling guilty and being guilty. The enemy wants us to feel guilty about everything.) We must keep a clear conscience and not play games with God. If the Lord points out sin when we come before Him, we can get it cleaned out of our lives through sincere repentance, then approach the throne of God with clean hands and a pure heart.

Psalm 66:18

_____

Psalm 24:3–4

_____

_____

_____

Coming to the Lord with a clean heart includes making sure our relationships with others are right before we come to the Lord.

Acts 24:15–16

_____

_____

Matthew 5:23–24

_____

_____

Interruptions. Think ahead to avoid as many potential interruptions as possible before you begin your prayer time. Take the phone off the hook, put a sign on the door, or ask your family to give you some time alone. You may find it easier to go for a walk or a drive instead of praying at home. Despite all your precautions, you will still have interruptions. It's just a part of the battle, so start up again where you left off and don't give up. God doesn't get frustrated when things distract us or interrupt our time with Him. He knows more than we do that prayer is a battle.

A feeling of dryness. You may not feel much when you pray. It's easy to hear other Christians' testimonies about how close they feel to the Lord or how they get tingly goose bumps each time they pray, and to feel left out if your experience is less dramatic. Learn this now—don't expect awesome, glamorous things to happen *while* you're praying. Expect them to happen *because* you pray! The Lord is listening, regardless of the state of your emotions.

Psalm 34:15

_____

_____

Knowing this is a stand of faith and will keep you from discouragement. God has the sovereign right to do things in His own timing, which is usually different from ours. The incredible visitations of God's Presence and the times He has spoken very clearly to me have usually not occurred during my prayer times. Instead, they have been while I'm driving, during worship, or when the Lord wakes me up in the middle of the night. Pray by faith and leave the response to Him. The worst thing we can do is say, "Okay, God, You have fifteen minutes to speak to me."

Despite your feelings, your consistent prayer is pushing back the forces of darkness and calling in the power of God. The devil would love for you to believe that nothing is happening, but both angels and demons move when we pray. We are blinded to the spiritual dimension unless God allows us to see into it, but that dimension is real and will be affected by our prayers. Read 2 Kings 6:13–17 for a great story about this.

Waiting for the Answers to Prayer

Earlier we mentioned Satan's strategy to attack our prayer lives. Satan's first area of attack is to keep us from praying, and his second is to hinder God's answer from arriving. Read Daniel chapters 9–10 to see more of what is happening in the spiritual realm. Daniel had been fasting and praying for three weeks without results. How many of us would have given up? Finally, an angel appeared with an incredible story. He told Daniel that God had sent him as soon as Daniel had begun praying but a demonic "prince" had prevented him from getting through. The angel had had to send for reinforcements. After winning that battle, he delivered the message to Daniel, and he would have to fight on his way back to heaven. Sounds like a Frank Peretti novel!

Faith is the channel through which God sends the answers to our prayers. Let's "fight the good fight of faith" (1 Timothy 6:12) until we see the fruit of our prayers. Sometimes we give up and draw back in discouragement when it appears that God is ignoring our prayers. What if the answer we are hoping for is on its way?

Hebrews 10:35–39

_____
_____
_____
_____

TRUE STORY

In January of 1985, I awoke at 3:00 AM after a strange dream and began to ask the Lord what the dream meant. God spoke some amazing revelation to me, and I recall thinking, "Wow! I'll have to write it down tomorrow." Then the Lord said, "Get up and write it down now. By tomorrow it will all be gone." I got up and had three incredible hours of praying and writing what the Lord showed me. From that early morning came my life messages in ministry: the value of souls, the reality of eternity, and Christians' need to die to self. I'm so glad I got up and wrote it down!

You may at first see blessing and immediate answers to prayer. God will frequently send these to encourage our commitment to a real prayer life. Then comes the phase of testing, with few answers to prayer and no sense of God's Presence at all. This is when faith really grows, so don't give up. Press on!

Practical Keys to a Powerful Prayer Life

Here are some ways to move forward in developing a fruitful habit of prayer.

1. Obey God's leading in the length of your daily prayer times. As your walk with Jesus grows, the time you are now spending with Him won't be enough. Right now, you might not be able to think of enough things to pray about for an hour, but later you'll be amazed at how quickly an hour will go by. At the same time realize that God is impressed not by the length of your prayers but by the quality of those prayers.

Ecclesiastes 5:2–3

_____

_____

_____

Matthew 6:7

_____

_____

2. Pray when the Holy Spirit comes upon you, even if it isn't your regular time with God. Of course, as we discussed in the first part of this teaching, you can have fellowship with God all day long. There are times when God will lead you to drop what you're doing for intense intercession or spiritual warfare or simply to share His burden with you. At these times, you'll find prayer especially powerful and fervent.

3. Keep pen and paper handy every time you pray. This is very important. God will remind you of people and responsibilities you've forgotten, point out priorities, and give you Scripture to meditate upon.

4. Pray specifically, not generally. Let the Holy Spirit focus your prayers and target them according to His plan.

5. Pray what's in your heart, not what's on your lists. Prayer lists can make your prayer mechanical and dull. They can be useful to remember people or places, but God wants passion in our prayers and fervency in spirit. Never just go through the motions.

James 5:16

_____

_____

Romans 12:11

_____

_____

Go pray some prayers that will have powerful effects!

Application

1. Have you ever had your priorities out of order (Mark 3:14), trying to do something for God without first being in right relationship with Him (Mark 3:13)?

2. How much of your prayer life revolves around your own personal needs?

3. Which of the hindrances to prayer usually happen to you?

Follow-Up

1. Have you encountered a spiritual battle to hinder your prayer life this week?

2. Which of the hindrances to prayer we discussed have happened to you this week?

3. Has the enemy stirred up personal problems in your life to try to make you focus your prayer life on yourself?

4. Has the Holy Spirit led you to intercede for others this week—friends, family, school, city, or nation?

5. Has the Lord shown you anything during your prayer times this week?

SCRIPTURE MEMORY

Galatians 6:10 Therefore, as we have opportunity, let us do good to all, especially to those who are of the household of faith.

Philippians 2:3–4 Let nothing be done through selfish ambition or conceit, but in lowliness of mind let each esteem others better than himself. Let each of you look out not only for his own interests, but also for the interests of others.

FILL OUT BOOK REPORT 1 ON THE NEXT PAGE.

DAILY BIBLE STUDY

✓ Check when completed		
Sunday	John 1–2	____
Monday	John 3–5	____
Tuesday	John 6–8	____
Wednesday	John 9–12	____
Thursday	John 13–17	____
Friday	John 18–21	____
Saturday	Acts 1–4	____

BIBLE-READING QUESTIONS

_____
_____
_____
_____
_____
_____
_____
_____
_____

PRAYER NEEDS THIS WEEK

_____
_____
_____
_____
_____
_____
_____
_____
_____
_____
_____

4

Book Report 1

Title of book: _____

Author: _____

Did you like it?

_____
_____

Would you recommend it to others?

_____
_____

What impressed you most about this book?

_____
_____
_____
_____

How did God use the book to speak to you?

_____
_____
_____
_____

Other comments or thoughts about the book:

_____
_____
_____
_____

Lesson four
CHANGED INTO HIS IMAGE: SERVANTHOOD

Many Christians think that spiritual growth is learning more facts about God. This is only the beginning. God doesn't want us to learn *about* Him as we would learn about math or history. He wants us to *know* Him. If all we have is head knowledge of rather than a growing love relationship with God, we have missed out and may become proud (1 Corinthians 8:1).

GOD'S GOAL FOR US

God's goal for us is to become like Jesus. We'll never become a member of the Trinity or be the Lord and Savior, but God's work in our lives is restoring in us the image of God that sin has ruined.

Genesis 1:26–27

_____

_____

_____

Jesus explained this to the Pharisees in Matthew 22:15–22. He told them that since the Roman coins showed the image of Caesar, the coins belonged to Caesar. Because humans bear the image of God, they belong to God. However, sometimes the image of God is so corrupted by sin that it's hard to imagine it's still there. The whole process of redemption is God's plan for restoring corrupted human beings to what they should be and placing them back into a relationship with Him. Since Jesus is the perfect example of what a person should be (as well as being Almighty God), He is the pattern for God's work in our lives.

Romans 8:29

_____

_____

2 Corinthians 3:18

_____

_____

Every day many influences compete to affect our motives, priorities, goals, and values. Is the Lord changing you into His image?

Romans 12:2

_____

_____

SHOWING JESUS TO THE WORLD

One of the Lord's goals as He transforms us into the image of Jesus is that we would show the world who He is. This is a parallel between our lives and the life of Jesus. Jesus showed the world what the Father is like. Anyone who wants to know the character of God can look at Jesus to see it.

Hebrews 1:3

_____

_____

John 14:9

_____

_____

Just as Jesus shows the world what the Father is like, Christians have the responsibility to show the world what Jesus is like. Scripture shows that God places this daunting duty in our hands.

John 9:5

_____

_____

Matthew 5:14

_____

_____

As God works in our lives, we show more of the character of Jesus. The world desperately needs to see living examples of who Jesus is and what He is like. Just as in Jesus' time, people today are looking for the reality of God and trying to find Him.

John 12:20–22

_____

_____

_____

The unsaved world frequently hears about Jesus but doesn't see Him. The Lord isn't still living in a human body. We are His Body here on earth. When the men in this passage wanted to see Jesus, they came to the disciples. It was easy for the disciples to point out Jesus. People still want to see Jesus, and they come to His present-day disciples. We must show Jesus to them through our lives.

While on earth, Jesus limited Himself to the form of a man. He was all of God living in a human body. When He was in Capernaum, He wasn't in Bethlehem. When He was in Jerusalem, He couldn't be in Nazareth. God's Presence is everywhere (Jeremiah 23:23–24; Psalm 139:7–10), but Jesus' physical presence was restricted to one place at a time. His life expressed the nature and character of God to humankind. Jesus said, "It is to your advantage that I go away" (John 16:7). How could that be? Now that He has risen, ascended into heaven, and sent His Holy Spirit to the Church, every disciple can show the nature and character of God. People in Buenos Aires, Boston, Berlin, and Beijing can all see a living example of the Presence of God at the same time if Christians live it in front of them. As much as the Father accomplishes His goal to make us into the image of Jesus, the world can see Him. Many people have never read the Bible and never will, but they read our lives every day. Are we faithfully showing Jesus to the world?

2 Corinthians 3:2–3

_____

_____

_____

_____

How Do We Get There?

The process of transformation involves several essential elements besides learning more facts about God.

Discipline. This includes both God's correction and our responsibility to keep our own lives in line with God's Word, which is self-discipline.

Hebrews 12:5–11

_____

_____

_____

_____

_____

1 Corinthians 9:27

_____

_____

_____

A part of discipline is learning to endure hardship. No one looks forward to difficult circumstances, but such circumstances can cause us to rely on the Lord for strength, and our faith grows as a result.

2 Timothy 2:3–7

_____

_____

_____

_____

TRUE STORY

Our first mission outreach to Nicaragua took place just a few years after civil war, an economic collapse, and a communist dictatorship devastated the country. We were surprised to see so little of the upbeat *fiesta* mentality found in the rest of Latin America. The beaten-down people walked silently through the streets, looking at the ground. Whenever our mission team walked toward them, the people stepped off the narrow sidewalk into the gutter to allow us to pass. As soon as I realized that this was happening and I spoke to our team about it, the team agreed to take a small but significant step to honor the people and show them that we had come to serve and didn't think we were any better than they were. From that day on, we were the first to step into the gutter and allow the Nicaraguans to stay on the sidewalk. God blessed us with an incredibly fruitful outreach. Could our commitment to lower ourselves, literally and spiritually, have opened up both the favor we had with the people and the blessings of the Lord?

Death to self or denial of selfishness. Out of love for the Lord and a desire to please Him, we place His will above our own. As the Scriptures teach us and as the Holy Spirit leads us, we do what we don't want to do and don't do what we want to do. This is foundational to being a disciple of Jesus.

Matthew 16:24–25

_____

_____

_____

We must count the cost of following Jesus. We recognize that rebellion against His will causes us to lose intimate fellowship with God. We can grieve the Holy Spirit and disqualify ourselves from being useful to Him.

Ephesians 4:30

_____

_____

2 Timothy 2:20–22

_____

_____

_____

Suffering. Like it or not, this is a required course in God's curriculum. Jesus set the example by going down this path before us.

Hebrews 2:10

_____

_____

Hebrews 5:8

_____

_____

1 Peter 2:21–24

_____

_____

_____

_____

The Greek word for _example_ literally means "tracing." Think of your life as a blank sheet of paper. Countless options are available to you as you go through life. You can draw the plan of your own design or choose to trace Jesus' life. This is the pattern God calls us to follow. God doesn't send trials and suffering needlessly. He has a divine purpose for every problem we face in life.

James 1:2–4

_____

_____

_____

Romans 8:18

_____

_____

_____

1 Peter 4:12–14

_____

_____

_____

2 Corinthians 4:17

_____

_____

_____

1 Peter 5:10

_____

_____

_____

TRUE STORY

The Chavita neighborhood in Juarez, Mexico, was poor, gang-infested, drug-saturated, and filthy. Our mission team of 150 spent a week helping the missionary there. We saw that the soccer field in the midst of a trash dump was a key community gathering place. While the rest of the group did construction and children's evangelism, about ten young people and adults filled a truck and a huge trailer with mountains of dirty diapers, tires, broken appliances, ragged clothes, and assorted garbage. Can you imagine the odor? The work was exhausting and dirty, but we finished with a great sense of accomplishment and built bleachers where the trash had been. To this day, the area around the bleachers has stayed clean, and our labor showed an important witness to the community.

Many times, we want the result of spiritual growth without paying the price for it. An easy, soft life cannot produce strong disciples. You've heard the expression "no pain, no gain." If we want the Lord to transform us into the image of Jesus, sometimes it's going to hurt.

THE GOAL OF DISCIPLESHIP: BECOMING A SERVANT

True discipleship can lead in only one direction: becoming like Jesus.

1 John 4:17

_____

_____

From time to time, we meet Christians who are different from everyone else. They have allowed the work of the cross in their lives through discipline, death to self, and suffering, and now their lives show Jesus to a far greater degree than do ours. Even being around them is convicting, because we are aware that they are living on a level of obedience, holiness, and purity of heart that we don't know. Their genuineness is a constant testimony to the world. Do you know anyone like this? Could you name more than a few of this type of believer? Would you like to be one? Like Jesus, they are servants. We can't share in Jesus' role as Savior or Redeemer, but God calls us to share in His role as Servant.

Isaiah 42:1

_____

_____

Isaiah 53:11

_____

_____

Philippians 2:5–8

_____

_____

_____

_____

As the Lord changes us into His image, we will become less selfish and more willing to serve others.

Galatians 5:13

_____

_____

This is the opposite spirit from the world's perspective. Most people want to be served, not serve others. Mankind usually thinks, "What's in it for me? How can I get more? How can I make it to the top?" The world's motive is grabbing, but the kingdom's motive is giving. Can you picture how different the world would be if everyone wanted to give? Then everyone would also be receiving! What if people were always asking themselves, "How can I make someone's life easier? How can I make others happier?" Life in this world would be so very different.

Galatians 6:10

_____

_____

If you want to be great in God's kingdom, lay down your rights and serve others. If you want to be the greatest, become a slave with no rights at all.

Matthew 20:25–28

_____

_____

The best judges of our servanthood are the people who live with us. They know what we're really like. If you want to know how much of a servant you are, ask your mother. For those of you who live away from your family, ask your roommate. How much self-sacrifice do others see in your life, and how much selfishness? God's call to servanthood will have a different application for each of us. He will call each of us to some form of laying down our life for others. Jesus is the ultimate example of this.

John 15:12–13

Mark 10:45

Matthew 16:25

If we try to keep our lives for ourselves, we lose our life. This doesn't mean physical death. Many believers find that after an exciting start in their Christian lives they drift into boring religiousness. They have missed the adventure of living in the middle of what God is doing. As they are slowly molded into the world's ways, they fail to seek a place to serve and don't take steps of faith. By not laying down their lives they lose the life they could have in Jesus. Don't fall into this trap!

The Rewards for Being a Servant

A release of joy comes when we take steps of faith to fulfill God's call to serve (Luke 10:17). As we lay down our lives for the Lord and others, we find real life. There's no deeper satisfaction than being in the center of God's will. This is far more than happiness. Happiness comes from what happens. When good things happen, we have happiness, but when bad things happen, we lose happiness. Joy comes from God's approval, and we can find it only in His Presence.

Psalm 16:11

God promises eternal rewards for His servants. We will receive these crowns when we stand before Him one day (1 Corinthians 9:25; 2 Timothy 4:8; James 1:12; 1 Peter 5:4; Revelation 2:10). As we serve Him faithfully, we can be assured that we are fulfilling His purpose for our lives. He has planned both the ways that we show Jesus to the world by serving and the rewards that come as a result. Some people fail to serve and then miss their reward in heaven. If you cooperate with the Lord as He transforms you and you become His servant, He won't have to find someone else to do your job, and that person won't receive the reward He had planned for you. You'll receive the reward yourself. The obedient receive the crowns.

Revelation 3:11

_____

_____

For all of us who love and serve Him, Scripture holds a promise: "Then those who feared the LORD spoke to one another, and the LORD listened and heard them; so a book of remembrance was written before Him for those who fear the LORD and who meditate on His name. 'They shall be Mine,' says the LORD of hosts, 'on the day that I make them My jewels. And I will spare them as a man spares his own son who serves him.' Then you shall again discern between the righteous and the wicked, between one who serves God and one who does not serve Him" (Malachi 3:16–18).

APPLICATION

1. How do people see the Presence of God in your life?

2. Describe how God's tools for molding us into the image of Jesus are working in your life.
   a. discipline

   b. self-denial

   c. suffering

3. How has your life traced the example of Jesus (1 Peter 2:21–24)?

4. Give a recent example of how you have placed God's will above your own.

FOLLOW-UP

1. How has the Lord been transforming you into the image of Jesus this week?

2. What is one way you have shown the character of Jesus to people around you this week?

3. What is one way you have been a servant to your family this week? How about at school or at work?

4. Have you found a release of joy by being a servant?

5. How have you laid down your rights and died to self this week?

SCRIPTURE MEMORY

Romans 14:7–9 For none of us lives to himself, and no one dies to himself. For if we live, we live to the Lord; and if we die, we die to the Lord. Therefore, whether we live or die, we are the Lord's. For to this end Christ died and rose and lived again, that He might be Lord of both the dead and the living.

2 Corinthians 5:15 And He died for all, that those who live should live no longer for themselves, but for Him who died for them and rose again.

WRITE YOUR SALVATION TESTIMONY (3–5 PAGES). REFER TO PAGE 15 FOR INFORMATION.

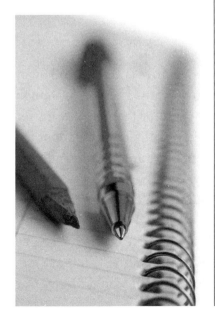

DAILY BIBLE STUDY

✓ Check when completed		
Sunday	Acts 5–8	_____
Monday	Acts 9–11	_____
Tuesday	Acts 12–15	_____
Wednesday	Acts 16–18	_____
Thursday	Acts 19–21	_____
Friday	Acts 22–25	_____
Saturday	Acts 26–28	_____

BIBLE-READING QUESTIONS

_____
_____
_____
_____
_____
_____
_____
_____
_____
_____

PRAYER NEEDS THIS WEEK

_____
_____
_____
_____
_____
_____
_____
_____
_____
_____
_____

5

Lesson five

Whose Life Is It, Anyway? (Surrender)

When you go to a grocery store, you find many brands to choose from. In a restaurant, you can order your eggs, tacos, or pizza lots of different ways. The ice cream shop offers many flavors. We have numerous choices available and the opportunity to pick what we want and reject what we don't like. Unfortunately, many people take the same approach to Christianity, choosing to follow the Lord as though they were at a salad bar. Do we take two helpings of blessings and pass on the obedience?

Two Kinds of Christians

Christians have two very different perspectives about how to relate to the Lord. One is a haughty, overconfident view that emphasizes what God wants to do for us. The other is a humble view, emphasizing what we must do for Him. Let's see what the Bible says about this.

Romans 14:7–9

_____

_____

_____

In verse 8 Paul says, "We are the Lord's." A tiny punctuation mark makes all the difference in the world, because it shows the two kinds of lives Christians live. That tiny apostrophe shows that we belong to the Lord. It turns the word *Lords* into a possessive noun. We are not the Lords, plural. We are the Lord's property. Let's look at another place that shows this:

1 Corinthians 6:19–20

_____

_____

_____

That little apostrophe is there again, showing that the Lord bought us with a price and now God owns us. Yet many Christians live as though *they* are the Lord and God is their servant. They act as though God exists to answer their prayers according to their own selfish desires. Faith for them is a means for all of their wishes to come true rather than a means of extending the kingdom of God throughout the world. Some preachers go so far as to say we are little gods—what arrogance! We aren't gods, and we'll never become gods. We're not in charge. He is!

The theology of redemption is that man's guilt was far greater than he could ever repay to God through religious efforts or good deeds. The Lord saw this, and since He loves us, He took upon Himself the cost of bringing us out of our sins and back to Him. In the Old Testament, He taught the people to sacrifice a spotless lamb for their sins as a forerunner for the time when Jesus, the Lamb of God, would die for humankind. The lamb's blood represented the Lamb's blood, which would forgive our sins and purchase us for God.

Leviticus 17:11

_____

_____

_____

Acts 20:28

_____

_____

_____

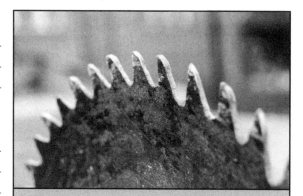

If we claim the blood of Jesus to forgive our sins and save us, we need to realize that the same blood paid for us, and now God has absolute right to us. We're His property. We can't do whatever we want with our lives, because these are not our lives anymore—they are His.

This may sound impersonal to some people. The idea of God's owning us doesn't sound very loving. It's true that our relationship with Him is that He is our Father and we are His sons and daughters. God has adopted us into His family. Yet when it comes to His will and commandments, God is also our Ruler and King. We can't have one without the other. We can't ignore the fact that the blood purchased us here and now, and then take the blood and apply it to heaven so that one day we can enter there.

We have never lived our own lives or been our own person. Before we came to Jesus, we were slaves to sin and to the devil. Every rebel thinks, "I'm doing my own thing. Nobody can tell me what to do. I live the way I want to." He or she is deceived. Every rebel is doing the *devil's* thing. We were slaves before, controlled and ruled by sin and by the enemy. Now we have the kindest, most loving Master in the universe.

THE BATTLE BETWEEN FLESH AND SPIRIT

If there is any conflict between your will and God's will, it is over this point: whose life is it, anyway? The fundamental battle between flesh and spirit ends here. Does the Lord have absolute right to *every* aspect of your life, or are there parts you have reserved for yourself?

Either we think we're still the lord of our lives and reject Jesus' rightful place as Lord, or we surrender to Him and live as real Christians. Is my life still mine, or is it His? If He owns me, everything in my life is His: my

TRUE STORY

When our son was about five years old, he liked to come out to the garage and watch me fix things with my tools. One day he asked if he could use my electric saw. Knowing how dangerous that would be for a small child, I told him no. His big blue eyes filled with angry tears. He protested, "But I know how! I'll be careful! I won't get hurt!" I tried to convince him that I had good reasons for refusing to let him use the saw, but he was too upset to listen and too young to understand. Was I just a mean father denying my son legitimate fun, or was my love for him the motivation to keep him far away from what could easily destroy his life? This is how it is with the Lord. Sometimes we don't understand His will, but it's always rooted in love for us. My son could have waited until I was asleep one night, snuck into the garage, and started up the saw, but the results could have scarred him for life or killed him. I'm glad that he never tried. Now, at age twenty-one, he can use the saw anytime he wants to. I would even be happy to buy him his own saw for Christmas. We may try to sneak behind God's back and do what He has forbidden, but there's tremendous risk in it for us. Isn't it better just to trust Him and wait for His approval?

time, talents, possessions, money, desires, career, education, relationships, and plans. No one has the right to say, "Sorry, Lord, I know what You want, but this is what I want."

Luke 6:46

_____

_____

If your time belongs to Him, you can never say, "I'm too busy to do something for God." If your possessions belong to Him, you'll be willing to let go of them when He leads. If your talents belong to Him, so does the choice in how you use them and the results of having those talents. Can you picture the servant in Jesus' parable (Matthew 25:20) saying, "Look, Lord! With the five talents you gave me, I earned five more. Two for You and three for me." What would the Lord think of that? "Well, Lord, how about three for You and two for me?" No! It all belongs to the Lord. If your life belongs to Him—and someday He even asks for that—He owns it, doesn't He?

Revelation 12:11

_____

_____

We can't live as though the Lord is interfering with our desires and plans. Many Christians want God's Presence in their lives, just off to the side but within arm's reach, close enough to help them when trouble comes but not getting in the way of their plans. This is so very different from a Christian who has surrendered his or her will to the Lord and just wants to follow Him.

Psalm 16:8

_____

_____

Often we think about our lives as though we still owned them: "I want this, I'm going here, I'm doing that. These are my goals. This is mine." We live independently and even pray as though God were our servant, on call to help us and give us whatever we ask for. Note the perspective of the disciples in the following scripture. If Jesus does whatever we ask, who is the master, and who is the servant?

Mark 10:35

_____

_____

The Lord is neither a genie in a bottle nor Santa Claus. He isn't there to fulfill our plans. We are here to fulfill His plans. He is Lord! We can't give Him a narrow range of possibilities and say, "Show me Your will as long as it is within these limits." Every option must be open to Him. We can't say, "No, Lord." Those words don't fit in the same sentence. We can't reserve the right to obey Him when His will agrees with ours but ignore His commandments when they are difficult or uncomfortable.

Matthew 16:24

_____

_____

_____

If the Lord were a tyrant or a dictator, we might have reason to grumble about His commands or disobey what we perceive to be His unreasonable expectations. Yet Scripture makes it clear and our own experience shows that God commands only what is best for us. He made the laws to protect people from harming themselves and others. There are no arbitrary rules, made just because God felt like showing off His authority. No laws exist that are designed to frustrate or torment us by withholding any good things from us. God's will and His expectation that we will obey it provide for man's safety from the destructive results of sin. God loves us too much to let us do whatever we want.

1 John 5:3

_____

_____

Psalm 84:11

_____

_____

_____

Deuteronomy 10:12–13

_____

_____

_____

_____

Understanding His goodness and the reasoning behind His will makes obeying Him so much easier. However, our stubborn flesh still fights against God's right to our lives. The truth is that we're not in the position of negotiating with Him when He wants one thing and we want something else. We have no right to compromise on some middle-ground solution. The Lord Jesus Christ deserves total and immediate obedience, not

TRUE STORY

I recall two of the most significant times of my own surrender to the Lord. The first was as a new believer at age seventeen, when I kept realizing how many things in my life were displeasing to the Lord. All the non-Christian music went first. Next, I got a big, black, plastic garbage bag and searched through my room, tearing the rock band posters from my walls and tossing occult books, pornography, off-color humor, and anything else that might offend the Lord. I knew that a halfway commitment to being a Christian wasn't enough.

A few years later, while serving as a youth pastor but resisting a call to missions that terrified me, I realized that it was time to stop fighting. We had watched a movie called *Peace Child* in a Bible-school class, and I had been deeply touched. Going outside with tears streaming down my face, I said, "Lord, I'll go where You send me and do what You tell me." That simple statement of surrender has been my prayer for the past twenty-plus years as I've had adventures with God in nineteen countries, ministered in the largest churches in several nations, been on national television in several countries, and watched thousands come to Jesus. It's still my prayer. Will you make it yours, too?

foot-dragging, grudging compliance. If Jesus could give His life and blood for us, anything He asks of us is insignificant by comparison. The response of a Christian who understands these principles is joy and gratitude—we serve the Living God. When we grumble about having to obey, we dishonor Him. Whether our disagreements with the will of God are over what we'll do today or what we'll do for the rest of our lives, the root is the same. We are not relating to God out of love, and we think this life still belongs to us.

Have we put limits on what God can tell us to do? Inflexible boundaries or parameters? We can't bluff God with a surrender that's only on the outside. What if He comes to collect?

WHICH SIDE IS WINNING THE BATTLE IN YOUR LIFE?

Are you living for yourself or for the Lord? Here's the author's life Bible verse. It explains in one sentence what being a Christian is all about: living for God and not for ourselves.

2 Corinthians 5:15

_____

_____

We should ask ourselves questions to see whether we're living for Him.

2 Corinthians 13:5

_____

_____

1. Do you make major decisions without consulting the Lord? Unsaved people have to make choices based on their limited human wisdom. That's too scary! We can't see far enough into the future to understand the outcome of our choices. At each point of major decision in our lives, we have only one good option: to prayerfully discover the will of God and then follow it. This way everything will turn out right, because God is a good God.
2. Are you here on the earth for your own enjoyment or for His glory? How often do you make decisions based on "Is it fun?"
3. Is the goal of your life selfish—comfort, pleasure, ease, and security—or bearing much fruit to honor the Lord?
4. Is serving the Lord something you get to do or have to do?
5. In a conflict between your will and His, who usually wins?
6. Why do you believe that God has given you the talents or abilities that you have? Are they for God's glory or for your own selfish gains: money, status, ego? Many people—including some rock stars, some entertainers, some athletes, and even some Christians—misuse their talents for these selfish reasons.

TWO SIDES TO THE CHRISTIAN LIFE

It's a little tricky to learn how to see our relationship with the Lord. We're His children, yet we're His slaves.

Romans 8:15–16

_____

_____

_____

1 Corinthians 7:22

_____

_____

We're expendable for the kingdom's sake yet precious to Him. Our lives are at His disposal, but He values us so much He would never dispose of us. We need to see our lives from both sides. When we do, it becomes much easier to obey God's leading, even in the things He asks that seem the hardest or scariest. When we know His nature and character, we know we can trust Him. Steps of faith into the unknown aren't terrifying, since He will be there with us. Like Abraham, we know that even if He asks us to sacrifice what is most precious to us, He will make everything work out in the end (Hebrews 11:17–19). You can trust Him enough to give Him all that you are.

APPLICATION

1. Have you realized before that God owns your life?

2. Put in your own words what it means for God to own your life.

3. Have you ever negotiated with God when He has shown you His will but it isn't what you want?

4. Have you ever dragged your feet and complained about God's will?

FOLLOW-UP

The following six questions from this week's teaching will help you see whether you are living for the Lord.

1. Do you make major decisions without consulting the Lord?

2. Are you here on the earth for your own enjoyment or for His glory? How often do you make decisions based on "Is it fun?"

3. Is the goal of your life selfish—comfort, pleasure, ease, and security—or bearing much fruit?

4. Is serving the Lord something you get to do or have to do?

5. In a conflict between your will and His, who usually wins?

6. Why do you believe that God has given you the talents or abilities that you have?

SCRIPTURE MEMORY

Mark 8:34–35 When He had called the people to Himself, with His disciples also, He said to them, "Whoever desires to come after Me, let him deny himself, and take up his cross, and follow Me. For whoever desires to save his life will lose it, but whoever loses his life for My sake and the gospel's will save it."

Romans 12:1–2 I beseech you therefore, brethren, by the mercies of God, that you present your bodies a living sacrifice, holy, acceptable to God, which is your reasonable service. And do not be conformed to this world, but be transformed by the renewing of your mind, that you may prove what is that good and acceptable and perfect will of God.

DAILY BIBLE STUDY

✓ Check when completed

Sunday	Romans 1–3	_____
Monday	Romans 4–5	_____
Tuesday	Romans 6–8	_____
Wednesday	Romans 9–11	_____
Thursday	Romans 12–16	_____
Friday	1 Corinthians 1–6	_____
Saturday	1 Corinth. 7–11	_____

BIBLE-READING QUESTIONS

_____
_____
_____
_____
_____
_____
_____
_____
_____
_____

PRAYER NEEDS THIS WEEK

_____
_____
_____
_____
_____
_____
_____
_____
_____
_____

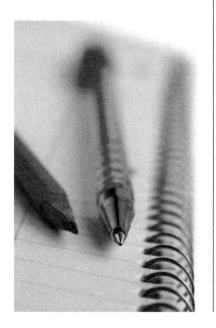

Lesson six

BROKENNESS

This may seem like an odd subject for those who have never heard the word *brokenness* related to our lives as Christians. Who would want to be broken? Doesn't Jesus put us back together? In this session, you'll see why brokenness is a good thing.

A COMMON PROBLEM

Many Christians miss the relationship they could have with the Lord. They have skimmed over God's dealings and the truth of the Bible, yet they wonder why they don't experience the fullness of the Holy Spirit and the joy of walking with Jesus. They seem to have put a limit on the intimacy of their fellowship with God, and they aren't bearing much fruit. They are unfulfilled and sense little of the life of God within them. Remaining at a shallow and superficial level of the Christian life, they have a Bible full of underlined promises and blessings but intentionally overlook the hard things God says throughout Scripture. Because they lack reality, they find it easy to manufacture a substitute through emotionalism. An imitation intimacy develops when their "walk with God" takes place mostly at the level of feelings and goose bumps. Some drift into religious mediocrity and cease actively pursuing the Lord. They are content to remain in their current condition and don't desire to know more of God and His ways.

Other Christians avoid this spiritual wasteland and become determined to press on and know the Lord. They want to honor the Lord with their lives and bear much fruit. A yearning for greater reality drives them to seek Him. If you're in the second category, read on for keys to greater depth in your walk with the Lord.

THE DEALINGS OF GOD

God takes these dedicated ones and puts them on a path to the reality they seek and the fruitfulness that will come as a result. Spiritual fruitfulness includes Christlike character, which is the result of the Holy Spirit's work in our lives (Galatians 5:22–23), and the effects our lives have on the lives of others. When the Lord deals with the obstacles that limit our usefulness to Him, we'll bear much fruit.

John 15:8

_____

_____

Scripture illustrates this idea of brokenness through the process of pruning that enables us to bear more fruit.

John 15:1–2

_____

_____

_____

We are often shocked when we ask God to work in our lives, making commitments from the depths of our soul to love and obey Him, and then find troubles coming our way. Why doesn't God make everything easier for us? Wouldn't it make sense for Him to reward His dedicated servants with a smooth life, full of blessings? Why does the Lord seem to be coming toward us with a saw in one hand and pruning shears in the other?

The path to usefulness and Christlikeness is not an easy one. Jesus told us to follow Him, and then He went to the cross and into the tomb. Our desire to know Him takes us to both the cross and the tomb. Death has never been a goal for most of us, but unless we know the fellowship of His sufferings through death to self, we can't know the power of His resurrection.

Philippians 3:10

_____

_____

_____

Those who allow the work of death to take place find that resurrection soon follows. After the resurrection came Pentecost, when the Father poured out the Holy Spirit in the upper room (Acts 2). The order of these three events is critical: the cross and the tomb first; then the resurrection, or new life; then Pentecost. Christians frequently try to rush past the first to get to the "good stuff." God's plan doesn't work that way. We take people who have never been to the cross straight into the upper room, then wonder why there is no fruit and no lasting change in their lives. They

TRUE STORY

I met the Lord at age seventeen and started preaching at age nineteen. God gave me early successes, and the Christian school at our church put me in charge of the high school Bible class. I became one of the leaders in a youth meeting that drew about four hundred kids on Friday nights. Seeing fifty kids come up at the altar call the first time I preached convinced me I was destined for greatness, but I didn't know how to get there the kingdom way. Soon, all this went to my head (1 Timothy 3:6). Judgment came from my heart and mouth easily, and I often used words like *backslider* and *reprobate*. Personal ambition to be a famous preacher made me arrogant, and it was time for God's discipline.

One night I had a dream that signaled the beginning of a long season of brokenness for me. In the dream, I stood in the packed church, preaching a powerful message, but the response of the audience was more like that at a rock concert. People were throwing flowers and cheering. Girls were fainting. At the end, a thunderous roar of applause filled the church, and the current leader of the youth group stood up in the back row of the church. "The name of Vinnie has truly been exalted here tonight," he said sincerely and without a trace of sarcasm. Still dreaming, I felt a deep sense of how wrong things were, and then I woke up. Soon doors on my budding ministry began to close as the church leadership helped me learn some humility. It was several years before they opened again.

I've had several seasons since then of God's correction, every one of them painful, but each time God brought me into a greater awareness that it's all about Him, not about me. Each time, bigger doors have opened, and greater fruitfulness for God's glory has resulted. My personal ambition to greatness is dead. At least I hope so. Brokenness hurts, but I need it. It's the cross.

may have only a slight touch of the Holy Spirit, but we call them filled. This is so different from the experience of the early believers, who turned the world upside down.

Acts 17:6

_____

_____

We are as full of God's Spirit as we have room for Him. Brokenness makes room so that He can fill us. The old saying is true: as your cross is, so will your Pentecost be. The lower we go with the Lord, the higher He can take us.

1 Peter 5:6, 10

_____

_____

_____

Such ideas as death and brokenness aren't appealing to many Christians today, but they are the only path to power and fruitfulness. People avoid this type of teaching because they think it won't make them feel good. Preachers don't often preach it, because people don't want hard words. But this is the key to life.

John 6:60, 66

_____

_____

_____

2 Timothy 4:2–4

_____

_____

_____

Isaiah 30:10

_____

_____

DEATH AND LIFE

Brokenness is the process of death to self, with the result of God's life flowing out through us to others. Jesus is the greatest example of this principle, but the disciples and all great men and women of God through the ages have been down this path.

2 Corinthians 4:10–12

_____

_____

_____

1 Corinthians 15:31

_____

_____

John 12:24

_____

_____

The following defines what needs to die and what branches the Lord will cut off:

- the independent self-will that tells God no
- pride
- personal ambition to succeed, with the goal of making a name or a fortune for yourself
- every aspect of exalting your own desires above the will of God
- confidence in your own ability to make yourself a better Christian or accomplish spiritual results
- plans, goals, and even dreams that conflict with the destiny God has in mind for you
- reliance on your own strengths
- in a word: *selfishness*—the life that revolves around me instead of around Jesus

The following verse sums up the whole concept of what to do.

Luke 9:23

_____

_____

What does the cross look like for you? Your death to self may be accomplished as you draw closer to God in the midst of difficult circumstances: rejection from those you love, family problems, sickness, disappointment, being unappreciated, being battered by temptation you feel powerless to overcome, humiliation, failure, or making bad decisions. God may reveal to you in a moment of divine clarity how wrapped up in self and consumed by the pettiness of this world your life really is. You may go through situations that are attacks from Satan, reaping the consequences of your own mistakes or heavenly correction, or be unsure of what is going on. The result, however, is the same: your circumstances and situations bring you to a place of knowing that you are nothing without Him.

Your cross might include dealings with God that aren't related to sin at all: giving up career plans because you hear a call to full-time ministry, forsaking comforts and possessions because you hear a call to give, leaving security and safety to trust God, refusing to pursue the plans that others have for your life because you hear *God's* plans. The bottom line of such situations is that you make a serious choice to put God's will above your own and follow the more difficult path because it will please Him.

DEFINING SELFISHNESS

Many books exalt the selfishness that God calls sin. With the psychology that has invaded the Church, the self life that God says must go to the cross is kept alive, nurtured, and protected. For example, a common response in Christian circles to self-pity in others is, rather than calling people to repent, commiserating with them. "You poor thing! You had a rough childhood. Let's spend years in recovery, helping you learn to love yourself." Jesus never said to love *ourselves*—He says that we are to love our *neighbor* as we love ourselves. His point is that if we will love others as much as we already love ourselves we'll be doing well. Self-love can show up in some types of depression and self-absorbed pouting that says, "Other people aren't paying as much attention to me as they should. I need to be the center focus!"

Matthew 22:39

_____

_____

Ephesians 5:29

_____

_____

Although the world and often even the Church promote self, God says that self must die. The world's values of self-confidence, self-sufficiency, self-indulgence, self-respect, and self-pity are sin! The only kind of self that God agrees with is self-control.

Galatians 5:22–23

_____

_____

_____

Since such ideas are shocking to some people, let's look carefully at this point of denying self. The kingdom of God takes an entirely different approach to reaching the same goals the world's kingdom strives to attain (Matthew 20:25–27). Calling self-confidence a sin doesn't mean that Christians should be mousy, weak, and afraid. It means that Christians find their confidence in God through faith in His ability to achieve the results. This puts us in a far stronger place than if we try to stir up confidence in our own limited abilities. Self-sufficiency, self-indulgence, and self-respect are wrong because their center is I instead of He. Whose life is it, anyway?

Don't fall for the popular idea that you need high self-esteem. You may have heard people say, "I have low self-esteem," as though it were a disease equal to diabetes or leukemia. Often such people are fishing for pity, and that's exactly the opposite of the one treatment that will help them to get well: denying self and following Jesus. Self is a bottomless pit—instead of trying to fill yourself with good thoughts and feelings, let your value come from knowing how God sees you. Instead of focusing on yourself, turn your eyes toward Him. Instead of striving for independence, let your life be wrapped up in Him, and you'll find total satisfaction and fulfillment. Ultimately, the Lord will put all selfishness to the test with the unchanging standards of His Word.

Luke 20:18

_____

_____

God will deal with all sin and selfishness in the universe. You have the choice to do this voluntarily (fall on the rock) or resist and be judged (the rock will fall on you). Welcome the Lord's work and don't fight Him as He takes self from your main focus and puts Jesus in His rightful place in your life.

The Flow of God's Life

Death and the cross are difficult subjects, but remember that beyond them is waiting the promise of life. In 2 Kings 4:8–37, we see the story about a prophet who was full of God's life. When the mother of a boy who had just died came to Elisha for help, Elisha sent his servant Gehazi to carry his staff and resurrect the boy. It didn't work. Gehazi didn't have the life within him to give to the dead boy. (In fact, in the following chapter God judges Gehazi for lying and for greed by smiting him with leprosy.)

Elisha went to the boy's home and stretched himself over the boy's corpse. The boy came back to life! God's life had filled the prophet so much that it flowed out to touch others. The death from the boy didn't kill Elisha; the life from Elisha conquered death in the boy. Elisha was so full of life that even after he died, his bones had enough anointing to raise another corpse to life.

2 Kings 13:21

_____

_____

This dying world desperately needs the resurrection life of Jesus and the power of the Holy Spirit. Can God use you to give His life to it? Do you give off God's life, or do you take on the world's death?

Ephesians 4:17–18

_____

_____

_____

Obstacles to Dying to Self

When Jesus was being crucified, His enemies mocked Him, saying, "Come down from the cross" (Matthew 27:40). Our enemy the devil, sometimes assisted by well-meaning but deceived people, still tells us to come down from the cross. Here's what that means today:

- "Don't try so hard to serve God—other people don't."
- "Why give up your valuable free time to read the Bible?"
- "Just pray before eating—there's no need to waste hours in prayer."
- "You went to church *last* Sunday, and you're really sleepy this morning."
- "Anything good on TV Wednesday night? Skip that boring youth group!"
- "Why wait until you're married? No one else does."
- "Let someone else do the hard work for God."
- "Keep quiet about Jesus—do you want people to think you're weird?"
- "Take the easy way out."

Don't listen to the enemy's lies. Follow the path of countless disciples who have gone before you.

Revelation 12:11

_____

You're doing this every time you do any of the following:

- Drag yourself out of bed to pray and seek God early in the morning, even if you're tired (Mark 1:35).
- Go without food in fasting and prayer, crying out to the Lord despite the rumbling in your stomach (Matthew 6:16–18).
- Stand up publicly for Jesus, risking rejection, putting all popularity and desire to be accepted on the line (Psalm 107:2).
- Reject the temporary pleasures of sin (Hebrews 11:25–26).
- Refuse the devil access to your life (Ephesians 4:27).
- Yield your desires for marriage, career, financial success, and achievement to Lord, being willing to take a place of lowly service if that's what He chooses (Psalm 86:11).
- Give Jesus the right to make all your decisions, with no areas reserved to do what you want independently from Him (Proverbs 3:5–6).
- Live with the consistent choice to discover and follow His plans, not sometimes choosing God's will and other times choosing human reasoning or personal desires (Acts 20:24).

CONFIDENCE IN THE FLESH

Repentance means a change of mind about something: what we used to think was good we now see as bad because it goes against God's Word and His ways. Repentance involves rethinking our ways and turning to God and His ways. When God breaks us, it is more than repenting of our sins. It is repenting of having confidence in the flesh or trusting in our own strength apart from Him.

Psalm 39:5

_____

_____

Romans 7:18

_____

_____

John 6:63

_____

_____

We all have either the world's false belief that we "can do all things" or the biblical belief that we "can do all things through Christ who strengthens [us]" (Philippians 4:13). Jesus didn't exaggerate when He told us in John 15:5, "Without Me you can do nothing." No good spiritual results can come from fleshly activity, even if the activity looks religious.

John 3:6

_____

_____
_____

What do we have to offer this world? The world doesn't need just another doctor, lawyer, or executive. It already has plenty of those. The world does need more doctors, lawyers, and executives who are vessels of the Holy Spirit.

2 Corinthians 4:7

_____
_____
_____

The world doesn't need our intelligence, strength, or personality. It needs the Presence of God to flow from our lives. This is true even in Christian circles. The Church doesn't need our great voice or our speaking ability. Have you ever heard a singer singing about the Lord with great skill, yet the song doesn't touch your heart? At another time you might hear someone with less ability than the other singer, yet this person's song makes you weep. You have probably heard a preacher with forcefulness and knowledge of Greek and Hebrew but no anointing. Compare that to an untrained speaker whose words carry divine authority and power. The difference is that one communicates life and the other doesn't. You can very easily tell a broken man from an unbroken man. Just see whether he is full of himself or full of the Presence of God. All any of us has to offer the world and the Church is Jesus.

How Does God Break Us?

We may not realize that some of the difficulties that come our way are answers to prayer. We've said, "Lord, change my heart. Make me like Jesus. Use me." And He has responded with circumstances designed to mold us into His image.

Psalm 119:71

TRUE STORY

A major influence in my life was a missionary woman who ministered in a remote part of Mexico until age eighty-six. The last time I heard of her, she was 101 and retired in the United States. The amazing impact of her life on countless people is a testimony to over seventy-five years of walking with God through much sickness, persecution, and hardship. The woman radiated peace and trust in the Lord. On several occasions, I heard her use an illustration of the work of God in her life. She said, "Life is like a cup. You don't know what's in it until it is bumped and something sloshes out. Whatever fills the cup is what comes out, whether it's something sweet or something bitter."

We'll face bumps in life and find out what is really in our hearts. Before God deals with selfishness, what sloshes out will be anger, impatience, pouting, or other kinds of "it's all about me" thinking. As we allow the dealings of God, we'll be filled with Him and find life flowing out of us. When you are bumped and Jesus' character sloshes out, people around you will be amazed.

_____
_____

The process of breaking us is different for each person, but the result of brokenness is the same. God has designed for each of us a unique set of circumstances aimed at exposing and slaying the self-life within us. No one can go through brokenness for you or tell you an easy way to get beyond it. No one can predict the means that God will use to deal with you. Just as Jacob wrestled with the angel (Genesis 32:24–26), it will be you and God alone. Brokenness is an intensely personal thing.

God operates with surgical precision. He never uses unnecessary force, and His fatherly love for us guides His actions. Sometimes we'll cry out and beg Him to stop His dealings with us, to let up and just let us stay as we are, but is this what we really want? Let's hold on by faith and believe that everything He is doing is for our good. As my missionary friend once said, "The best educations are the most expensive, and few people get them." Is the Lord teaching you costly lessons? If so, He has chosen you for something special. Stop fighting, and don't drop out!

Lamentations 3:33

_____

_____

Romans 8:28–29

_____

_____

_____

When we understand what God is doing, we'll pray, "Father, thank You for every breaking experience. Thank You for teaching me to depend on You instead of myself. Thank You for the humiliations that crush my pride, for rejection and persecution that teach me to draw near to You, for being unappreciated so that I work for the praises of God rather than of men. Thank You for changing my heart, my motives, and my desires, for teaching me to value what is eternal instead of what is temporary."

APPLICATION

1. How have you experienced the process of God's work that leads to brokenness?

2. Have you believed the worldly philosophy of your "need" to have high self-esteem and to hold on to your life rather than lose it?

3. How is the life of God flowing through you?

4. How does the enemy try to keep you from brokenness by telling you to "come down from the cross" (Matthew 27:40)?

FOLLOW-UP

1. How has the life of God flowed through you this week?

2. Give an example of how you have placed God's will above your own this week.

3. Give an example of how you have died to self and had a release of God's life.

4. How has the Lord been teaching you not to rely on your own strength?

SCRIPTURE MEMORY

1 Corinthians 15:58 Therefore, my beloved brethren, be steadfast, immovable, always abounding in the work of the Lord, knowing that your labor is not in vain in the Lord.

Galatians 6:9 And let us not grow weary while doing good, for in due season we shall reap if we do not lose heart.

DAILY BIBLE STUDY

✓ Check when completed

Sunday	1 Corinth. 12–14	____
Monday	1 Corinth. 15–16	____
Tuesday	2 Corinthians 1–6	____
Wednesday	2 Corinth. 7–10	____
Thursday	2 Corinth. 11–13	____
Friday	Galatians 1–6	____
Saturday	Ephesians 1–6	____

BIBLE-READING QUESTIONS

_____
_____
_____
_____
_____
_____
_____
_____
_____
_____

PRAYER NEEDS THIS WEEK

_____
_____
_____
_____
_____
_____
_____
_____
_____
_____

7

Lesson seven
FAITH AND FAITHFULNESS

In this session, we'll be talking about faith and faithfulness. By faithfulness, we mean a stick-to-it consistency in following God's plan for our lives. It is our response to hearing a call, a promise, or an assignment from God. Each of us has a particular call of God—something He wants to do with our lives to affect the world. Have you heard a call yet?

SHOOTING STARS VERSUS BURNING BUSHES

Many professing Christians are like shooting stars or fireworks—a brief blaze of glory, and then they are gone. They do well for three weeks, two months, or a year but fizzle out after a miniwalk with God. Even unsaved people can seem for a while to be Christians, because the flesh has a lot to gain from appearing religious: smug feelings of self-righteousness, a sense of superiority over others, the idea that God owes them something, or the praises of people (John 5:41, 44)—not to mention the chance to meet cute girls or handsome guys at youth group!

God sees a lot of "goodness" but very little faithfulness in the world (Proverbs 20:6). Too many Christians find that their passion for God has burned out. We want to help you become a burning-bush Christian. Remember when Moses saw the bush that the fire couldn't consume? The bush didn't burn out, because the Presence of God, not the bush's twigs and branches, fueled the fire.

Exodus 3:2

_____

_____

The bush could have burned on forever because the fire's source was eternal. In the same way, God is able to keep us from burning out spiritually if we learn to rely on His strength.

THE PLACE OF FAITH

Without faith, it is impossible to please God (Hebrews 11:6). Faith is the foundation of our lives as Christians. It is confidence in both the written Word and the words God speaks to our hearts. Faith is our confidence that God's nature and character back up what He says.

Faith is necessary to be faithful. We must be convinced that we're following and fulfilling the will of God. Unless a deep, internal desire to please Him motivates us, we'll lose interest or find an easier path than living out the plan He has for our lives. Fleshly zeal fizzles out!

God's path isn't an easy one. It has many barriers to test our faith along the way. The flesh is lazy, stubborn, and rebellious; the world tells us we're crazy; and the devil does all he can to sidetrack, discourage, and destroy us. Even well-meaning Christians might not understand when we hear more than they have heard. Sometimes Christian students hear God's direction but find that their parents, even those who are believers, don't confirm what they are hearing. This is an obstacle to overcome, not a license to rebel! It is a test of faith on the journey of faithfulness to His revealed will. God is well able to change parents' hearts and confirm His direction through them, or use parents to correct their children when they are off track. The key is the condition of one's heart when facing this obstacle. Are you humble and teachable, or arrogant and proud? Are you submissive or rebellious?

Living by faith is like running a marathon, not a fifty-meter dash. Faithfulness is a life of endurance. Such a life is not easy, but the rewards of faithfulness are extraordinary. Faithfulness brings the promises of God to pass.

Hebrews 10:35–39

_____

_____

_____

_____

Our consistent believing and obeying will result in our seeing the manifestation of the dreams and kingdom goals that God has placed in our hearts.

Ecclesiastes 5:3

_____

_____

At times during a marathon, the runners feel that they can't go another step. All their strength is gone, and exhaustion overwhelms them. Runners call this "hitting the wall," and many quit at this point. But others keep on going. Somehow they find the strength to continue, and as they run, they get their second wind. Energy returns, and they complete the race. Christians hit the wall too, and many quit the race. This can happen in our personal walk with God and cause backsliding, or it can occur in our calling to serve the Lord. At that point we can draw on His strength to keep going. We can reach the finish line in heaven someday.

2 Timothy 4:7

_____

_____

THE OBSTACLES TO FAITHFULNESS

Many obstacles face us as we pursue a long-term, fruitful Christian life. With God's help we can overcome all of them.

Romans 8:37

_____

_____

2 Corinthians 2:14

_____

_____

TRUE STORY

The campus Bible study on Thursdays wasn't going well. Out of 2,500 students, only a handful came. When they remembered. When the lure of the twelve fast-food restaurants across the street didn't capture them. When they didn't have too much homework. I knew that the Lord wanted me to do this, so every week I brought my guitar and my Bible. Sometimes no one came, and I would just play guitar, worship, and pray alone. Sometimes I was mad—mad at the kids, mad at God for not sending the kids, frustrated at the seeming waste of time. Over a decade of campus ministry, we had highs and lows as the group would grow to thirty-five, then the key seniors would graduate, and the group would dwindle again.

Finally, a door opened. The school began a weekly class period for clubs and organizations. Our attendance boomed to a seventy-five-kids-per-week, standing-room-only crowd. On the very day that the Lord called me to leave my youth pastor role and launch into a faith missionary role with Youth With A Mission and King's Kids, we held an evangelistic rally in the cafeteria, and about five hundred students came. God's grace and the sense of His call fueled faithfulness, and God blessed the end of my campus ministry with an amazing sendoff.

Wanting an easy life. It's easy to continue in the revealed will of God as long as things are going smoothly. If we have immediate proof that we're on the right track and have instant success, we'll keep on. We'll also become spiritually soft and weak. Tough times make strong believers. In the Body of Christ, we have too many Cub Scouts and not enough marines. A missionary friend of mine once said, "Christians need to learn how to take a punch." Marines don't go through boot camp at Disneyland. They go to Parris Island, where conditions are intentionally tough to make *them* tough.

God calls us by many names in the Scriptures. We are His children, disciples, servants, and friends. Let's not forget that He also calls us soldiers. What hardships have you endured for the sake of the gospel?

2 Timothy 2:3–4

_____

_____

_____

_____

Wanting our rewards on earth. Sticking to the will of God, whether in our personal lives or in our calling, isn't easy. When the going gets tough, we need much more than external motivation or satisfaction here and now. Most of the fruit of faithfulness won't show up until heaven.

Hebrews 11:24–27

_____

_____

_____

_____

God promises eternal rewards to those who obey Him (Revelation 2:7, 11, 17, 26; 3:5, 12, 21), but even those promises won't be enough to motivate us to continue when the easiest thing would be to give up. We need more than promises of mansions in heaven or gold streets when all our emotions tell us to quit. We need that deep, internal desire to please the Lord, based on our love for Him, that propels our faith. All the splendor of heaven pales in comparison to someday seeing His face and hearing Him say, "Well done, good and faithful servant. Enter into the joy of your Lord." Note that Scripture says not just the Lord, but *your* Lord (Matthew 25:23). When people who live out the lordship of Jesus by faithfully serving Him get to heaven, they don't care whether or not the streets are gold. A park bench in heaven would be enough. Nor do they care about mansions. If their Lord is there, that's all they want. Just to be with Him forever, knowing that He is pleased with the fruit of their lives, will be the source of their ultimate peace and satisfaction forever.

Satan's main attack—discouragement. If the enemy can get us to look at the circumstances instead of the Lord, we'll sink just as Peter did when he walked on the water (Matthew 14:28–32). Because Jesus had told Peter to come, at first Peter was obeying and doing what we might consider to be humanly impossible. When Peter took his eyes off Jesus and saw the problems surrounding him, his faith collapsed, and the Lord had to rescue him. Isn't it great to know that even when we fail, God is merciful and will help us! If you step out by faith to do the seemingly impossible because the Lord has called you, expect some discouraging circumstances and storms to come as the enemy tries to get you to take your eyes off Jesus. God is your source of encouragement in times like these. He is keeping His eye on you, and you must keep your eyes on Him.

2 Chronicles 16:9

_____

_____

Just as in Eden, the serpent is still trying to make us question that God really speaks to us and that He is telling us the truth (Genesis 3:1–5). Satan uses discouraging thoughts and comments from others to make us feel that what we're doing is a waste of time, that it won't amount to anything, and that God isn't interested. If his question is "Has God really said?" the answer of faith is "God said it, I believe it, and that settles it."

Our ammunition in this battle, the "fight of faith" (1 Timothy 6:12), is the Word of God. It's worth marking the following verses in your Bible and memorizing them for the battles you'll face in this area. I've faced some very discouraging times, and these were the verses I'd quote to myself each day. God's Word really can encourage us.

1 Corinthians 15:58

_____

_____

Galatians 6:9

_____

_____

Psalm 37:4–7

_____

_____

_____

_____

Also read Psalm 42 and Psalm 43.

Three Kinds of Faithfulness

Look in Luke 16:10–12 for the three kinds of faithfulness:

"He who is faithful in what is least is faithful also in much; and he who is unjust in what is least is unjust also in much. Therefore if you have not been faithful in the unrighteous mammon, who will commit to your trust the true riches? And if you have not been faithful in what is another man's, who will give you what is your own?"

Faithfulness in what is little. God starts us out small in serving Him. None of us could handle the pride that would result if He started us out in big things.

1 Timothy 3:6

_____

_____

Don't despise the day of small beginnings (Zechariah 4:10). God may not tell you at first, "You're going to change Ethiopia forever." He may say, "Go to church early and help set up chairs." It's natural to want to wait for the big opportunities, but you'll never hear the lifetime call if you aren't faithful in the daily call.

Matthew 25:23

_____

_____

Here's a radical idea. God has a perfect plan for His kingdom to come and His will to be done on earth as it is in heaven. He chooses various Christians to fulfill different parts of that plan, giving them different gifts to accomplish their work. When one of His servants is unfaithful, does that part of God's plan fail? God still wants to accomplish it and will give the unused anointing to someone who is faithfully using his or her gifts. Unused gifts are out there, waiting for a qualified person to use them. We can't just ask God to give them to us, but we can be qualified to receive them if we're faithful in what we have now (Matthew 25:28–29). Then, if we have a deep and God-given desire for a particular gift to operate in our lives, we can ask for it.

1 Corinthians 14:1

_____

_____

Faithfulness in money. Earthly riches are the test for how much we can be trusted with spiritual riches. Do we hoard money or give it away to meet needs? Are we wise, or are we foolish, careless, and impetuous? Do we plan ahead and consider the consequences of our actions? Are we selfish, or are we servants? Whether or not God can trust us with His riches is proven by our actions in the natural realm.

Faithfulness in what is another's. Will we be servants to men and women of God, laboring where only God sees and appreciates our work? Or do we want glory and attention? Serving other leaders in their ministries is part of God's school of character building. It teaches us humility and patience. One large church in the United States starts all its potential young leaders in the maintenance department. As these young people mop, paint, and clean toilets, they learn God's lessons to prepare them for greater service in the future. If they were to refuse to serve in these lowly positions, the leaders would see that their character was not formed enough to be given spiritual responsibilities.

God will promote us as quickly as He can, but our willingness to be faithful right now can slow or stop His work in our lives. You'll only get as far in the kingdom as your faithfulness goes. Every great work of ministry began with a man or woman who heard from God and stuck with it. Every difficult, painful, heartbreaking setback forged the character each would need later on to lead the larger work. Without the struggles and a response of faithfulness, these people wouldn't have become the kind of people God could trust with greater responsibility. If you'll be faithful, you'll see the fruit.

Proverbs 28:20

_____

_____

God has a part, and we have a part. His part is to call and choose us. Our part is to respond and to be faithful. The limits of our future ministries are in our hands. Souls are at stake. Cultivate the gift of determination, and be a faithful servant.

Revelation 17:14

_____

_____

APPLICATION

1. How has the enemy attacked you with discouragement to try to keep you from being faithful?

2. Give an example of a time you took your eyes off the Lord and put them on the circumstances around you, as Peter did in Matthew 14:29–31.

3. Have you already seen the rewards of being faithful in some area of life?

FOLLOW-UP

1. How have you been faithful this week…
   a. in little things?

   b. in money?

   c. in what is another's?

2. Do you desire a particular gifting or anointing? How will you become qualified to receive it?

3. How do you feel about the saying "The limits of our future ministries are in our hands?" Is this true?

SCRIPTURE MEMORY

Isaiah 57:15 For thus says the High and Lofty One who inhabits eternity, whose name is Holy: "I dwell in the high and holy place, with him who has a contrite and humble spirit, to revive the spirit of the humble, and to revive the heart of the contrite ones."

John 3:30 "He must increase, but I must decrease."

DAILY BIBLE STUDY

✓ Check when completed		
Sunday	Philippians 1–4	____
Monday	Colossians 1–4	____
Tuesday	1 Thess. 1–5	____
Wednesday	2 Thess. 1–3	____
Thursday	1 Timothy 1–3	____
Friday	1 Timothy 4–6	____
Saturday	2 Timothy 1–4	____

BIBLE-READING QUESTIONS

_____
_____
_____
_____
_____
_____
_____
_____
_____
_____

PRAYER NEEDS THIS WEEK

_____
_____
_____
_____
_____
_____
_____
_____
_____
_____
_____

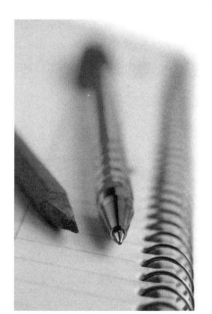

8

Lesson eight

HUMILITY

The issue of pride and humility is so important to the Lord that He draws back from the proud and comes near the humble. Pride is a sneaky sin—it's much easier to recognize it in others than in ourselves. Are you proud?

WHAT IS PRIDE?

One dictionary definition of *pride* is excessive self-esteem. A person who is proud is proud of something. Consider the following:

- talents
- accomplishments
- appearance
- possessions
- athletic ability
- friends
- spirituality
- intelligence
- Bible knowledge
- family
- spiritual gifts
- education
- personality
- musical ability
- wealth
- strength

And the list goes on.

Pride is never a secret sin—it always shows up in the way we treat others, such as arrogance or stepping on people around us, and in the way we talk about ourselves. Pride is evident in such common behavior as making people wait for us or clean up after us. Comparing ourselves with others is the basis of all pride.

2 Corinthians 10:12

_____

_____

We often measure various characteristics of other people and silently weigh their value on a scale like the one shown above. Our human tendency is to find areas where we can give ourselves a higher score, which boosts us up a notch in our own mental ratings. Then we look for flaws in other people's lives to lower those people a notch. This combination of pride and a critical attitude offends the Lord and harms our relationships with others.

THE SOURCE OF PRIDE

Pride comes when we find our identity and value in anything besides our relationship with Jesus. When a person's life centers on one of the temporary things listed previously, what happens if the person loses that thing? We've all seen or heard about people struck by tragedies that robbed them of the qualities on the list: successful executives who went bankrupt, beautiful women disfigured by a terrible accident, athletes confined to a wheelchair, and intelligent people who came down with Alzheimer's disease. Living based on any of these sources of pride is unstable. When a person knows that his or her value comes from God's unchanging love and acceptance through the blood of Jesus, that person will have security that he or she can depend on.

Pride is at the root of envy, judging, gossip, and many other sins. By keeping a humble heart, we can avoid a lot of trouble in our lives.

James 3:14–16

_____

_____

_____

_____

JOHN THE BAPTIST'S EXAMPLE OF HUMILITY

John the Baptist was a man sent from God to prepare the people for the coming of the Messiah. For a while, he was the most famous spiritual leader in the country (Matthew 3:5–6). Then it was time for Jesus to take His rightful place and for John to step down. John's followers came to John and tried to stir up pride and jealousy in him (John 3:26). John's response showed true godly character. His fame and influence were disappearing rapidly, but he knew what his role was: to point people to Jesus and not to himself. John knew who he was and who Jesus was. If he had been proud, he would have tried to keep the crowds for himself, but he showed genuine humility.

John 1:29

_____

_____

TRUE STORY

Are you like me, who usually learns thing the hard way? Knowing lots of Scripture about pride doesn't seem to keep it from rising up in my heart. God hates this and consistently reminds me to give Him the glory and not take personal credit in any area of life. When I had a small photo business going and started thinking that I was a really good photographer, equipment would break, jobs wouldn't come out, or the photo lab would ruin my film. I realized that I had to look to the Lord in every area and that I'm dependent on His blessing for things to go well.

When I started thinking I was a great driver, with lightning-fast reflexes and extraordinary road skills, I had several near accidents as a wake-up call. Once I was driving on a deserted road in New Mexico. For some unknown reason, my thoughts went to a man in our church who had recently told me that he had replaced the windshield in his car three times. I smugly thought about how my superior dedication brought the blessings of God in my life. May the Lord be my witness in this: at that exact moment, a rock flew up and cracked my windshield. There was no car ahead for a very long distance that could have sent that rock flying. The rock was a gentle reminder from the Lord to humble my heart.

_____

_____

John 3:30

_____

_____

Jesus later called John the greatest man ever born to a woman (Matthew 11:11). The lesson we can learn from John is not drawing attention to ourselves but pointing people to Jesus.

JESUS' EXAMPLE OF HUMILITY

If anyone deserves attention and honor, it is Jesus.

Colossians 1:18

_____

_____

Yet in submission to the Father's plan, Jesus refused to listen to temptations to draw attention to Himself in the wrong way and at the wrong time.

Matthew 4:5–6

_____

_____

_____

John 7:3–6, 8

_____

_____

_____

_____

Jesus did God's will in God's way and in His timing, showing Himself to be the ultimate example of humility.

Philippians 2:5–11

_____

_____

_____

_____

HOW GOD RESPONDS TO PRIDE AND HUMILITY

Jesus is the pattern for our lives as believers. Because of His humility, God exalted Him, and He will respond to us in the same way.

1 Peter 5:5–6

_____

_____

_____

When we humble ourselves before the Lord and before others, God steps in. When we exalt ourselves, He pulls back.

Psalm 138:6

_____

_____

James 4:6

_____

_____

1 Corinthians 1:29

_____

_____

If no flesh will glory in His presence (1 Corinthians 1:29), when we become proud, we lose the manifest Presence of God in our lives. It's as though the Lord says, "Think you're so great? Let's see just how well you do on your own." We sometimes have to learn the hard way that we're totally dependent on God. Pride is a manifestation of that independent self-life that must go to the cross. Our best features are not what make our lives worthwhile or valuable. The Lord is the treasure in our lives. We're just clay vessels that hold the treasure.

2 Corinthians 4:7

_____

_____

There is a right way and a wrong way to do anything. People who are proud and self-seeking often take shortcuts or ignore God's principles in their quest for fulfillment. They feel that rules that apply to others shouldn't apply to them. The consequences of pride and humility are polar opposites.

Proverbs 29:23

_____

_____

Proverbs 15:33

_____

_____

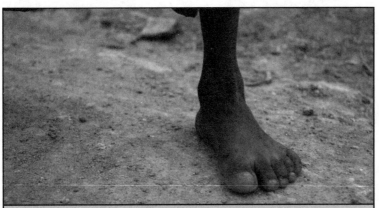

TRUE STORY

I love India, Indian people, and Indian food. My three outreaches in India were life changing. Each time I had opportunities to build bridges to the people by showing humility. The Hindu religion teaches that society has clearly defined levels called castes. This system is a racist and evil means of controlling others (the word *caste* means color). Many Indians believe that caucasian Americans belong to the highest caste because of their light skin, but obviously we are no better than anyone else.

During a conference for rural pastors, the leader asked if my friend and I would wash the feet of one hundred-plus pastors. This was easy for us to do, since we had gone to the conference as servants, and it was an important means of communicating our equality and respect for the Indian farmer/pastors.

While preaching at a much larger three-day citywide conference, I took advantage of every break to drink chai tea with the people. The people were amazed when I told them how much I liked the beverage and were shocked to hear that my wife had learned how to make authentic Indian chai during a trip to India and still makes it for our family. When our hosts served lunch and I ate Indian style, with no utensils and carefully using only my right hand (Indians use their left hand in place of toilet paper), they asked if I actually liked the food. When I said that I love their food and like to go to Indian restaurants in my country, a ripple of excitement went through the crowd that had gathered to watch the pale foreigner eat. Demonstrations of humility are a great way to build friendships.

Proverbs 16:18

_____

_____

_____

Those who try to exalt themselves find God actively working against them. In each person's ministry, the person can have his or her own personal ambition to greatness instead of developing the character of a servant, which is God's way to greatness. Self-promotion is a facet of pride and will get us into trouble. The way self-promotion backfires is that it can get us into realms of ministry or levels of responsibility where we're not supposed to be. If our character hasn't reached the point where God promotes us but we get where we are by human means, pride and a fall come naturally. The high road of self-promotion is the reason that some Christian leaders fall into sin and lose their ministry. Pride deceives these people to the point where they feel that the rules don't apply to them anymore or that they are too important for God to judge their sin. If we take the low road of humility in ministry, we'll get to the right place at the right time.

Psalm 75:6–7

_____

_____

_____

_____

In fact, every area of life works this way. Success and blessing come from following God's principles—humility, righteousness, faithfulness, and the fear of the Lord.

Proverbs 22:4

_____

_____

People in the world are going after riches, honor, and life, but they are ignorant of God's ways or are rebellious against Him. They want greatness but think that that means having many servants instead of serving many. Truly in God's kingdom the way up is down (Matthew 20:25–28).

THE FALL OF LUCIFER
The ultimate example of pride is Lucifer's fall from heaven.

Isaiah 14:12–15

_____

_____

_____

Lucifer's rebellion was rooted in pride and resulted in God's forcing him out of heaven.

Ezekiel 28:12–17

_____

_____

_____

_____

Jewels made up Lucifer's appearance, and they have beauty only by reflecting light. Lucifer, whose name means "light bearer," thought that he was beautiful in himself, without realizing that only the light of God made him beautiful.

1 John 1:5

_____

_____

He needed the light to be beautiful but was deceived into believing that He didn't need God. Even if Lucifer had been successful in trying to overthrow God (which never could happen), how beautiful would he be without God's light, living in total darkness? Not beautiful at all! Rebellion and pride are the basis of the desire to be independent from God. Before Lucifer became the deceiver, pride deceived him. The deceiver was deceived, and pride can have the same effect in our lives.

Obadiah 3

_____

_____

Pride always works hand in hand with deception. If people remain humble, they won't be deceived, but pride opens them up to believe lies (Genesis 3:4–5). In the same way, anyone who is proud is already deceived into believing that he or she is something apart from God. We see this in cults and religions that appeal to pride by teaching people that they can work their way to heaven and even become gods someday. This sounds great to the ego, but its root is from the father of lies.

John 8:44

_____

_____

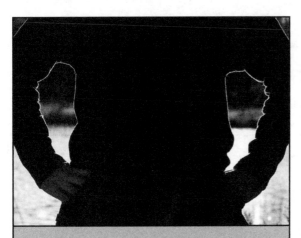

TRUE STORY

Here is a verse worth memorizing: "By pride comes nothing but strife, but with the well-advised is wisdom" (Proverbs 13:10). Whenever strife exists between people or even between nations, pride is the source. One or both parties involved are proud. We will always find Pride and its Siamese twin Stubbornness together. Whenever you and your friend, parent, spouse, or kids have a conflict, look for the twins. Because _we're_ proud, we tend to assume it's the other person who needs to repent of pride. Surely, the problem is the other person's, not ours! When my good friend got married and the pastor asked all of us seasoned husbands to give him a brief word of advice, mine was "Always be the first one to say I'm sorry." After twenty-five years of marriage, I'm still in need of this advice, as recently as, um, I hate to admit it...this morning. I'm sorry, honey. I love you!

Lucifer earned the name Satan, which means adversary. God threw him out of heaven and gave him a punishment that fit his crime. The one who wanted to exalt himself to the highest place will end up in the lowest place (Matthew 23:12). Beelzebub (Matthew 10:25; 12:24), which means the lord of flies, will live eternally surrounded by maggots and worms (Isaiah 14:11).

It's an interesting side note that occultists believe that Satan will defeat Jesus at the battle of Armageddon. Even Satan knows better than that, but the deception continues in the lives of his followers.

Revelation 12:12

_____

_____

_____

When we are proud, we fall into the trap Satan sets for us, following in his deception. None of us is immune to the temptation of pride—even King Saul fell because of it.

1 Samuel 15:17

_____

_____

_____

THE CURE FOR PRIDE

Since pride offends the Lord, how can we please Him?

Isaiah 57:15

_____

_____

_____

The cure for the deception of pride is the truth of God. All we have and all we are is a gift from God to us. We haven't earned anything. Maybe you've been faithful to develop a God-given ability, but that ability originated with God. Even wealthy people who think they are self-made received their abilities to accumulate wealth directly from God (Deuteronomy 8:18). God gave those gifts to us for His purposes, even though selfish use may corrupt them.

1 Corinthians 4:7

_____

_____

2 Corinthians 3:5

_____

_____

Romans 12:3

_____

_____

If we understand that everything we have has come from God, we'll give Him credit and not take credit ourselves. We'll be thankful instead of boastful. We'll ask Him how we can use our blessings and advantages to serve and glorify Him instead of serving and glorifying ourselves. Have you ever stopped to give God credit for every good thing in your life? What would your life be like without Him?

Jeremiah 9:23–24

_____

_____

_____

Application

1. Name one area of your life where you have found your identity and value. "I'm a great _____."

2. Have you used this area to draw attention to yourself or to God?

3. How can you gain more of the manifest Presence of God in your life?

Follow-Up

1. How have you found pride showing itself in your life this week?

2. Has pride tempted you to take shortcuts or ignore God's principles this week? Have you felt that some rules don't apply to your life?

3. Have you recognized that your strengths, gifts, talents, and abilities are a gift from God? Explain.

4. Are you making the transition from boastfulness to thankfulness?

DAILY BIBLE STUDY

SCRIPTURE MEMORY

Romans 6:6–7 [K]nowing this, that our old man was crucified with Him, that the body of sin might be done away with, that we should no longer be slaves of sin. For he who has died has been freed from sin.

1 Corinthians 10:13 No temptation has overtaken you except such as is common to man; but God is faithful, who will not allow you to be tempted beyond what you are able, but with the temptation will also make the way of escape, that you may be able to bear it.

FILL OUT BOOK REPORT 2 ON THE NEXT PAGE.

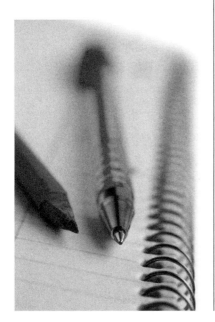

✓ Check when completed		
Sunday	Titus 1–3	_____
Monday	Philemon	_____
Tuesday	Hebrews 1–2	_____
Wednesday	Hebrews 3–4	_____
Thursday	Hebrews 5–7	_____
Friday	Hebrews 8–10	_____
Saturday	Hebrews 11–13	_____

BIBLE-READING QUESTIONS

_____
_____
_____
_____
_____
_____
_____
_____
_____

PRAYER NEEDS THIS WEEK

_____
_____
_____
_____
_____
_____
_____
_____
_____
_____

Book Report 2

Title of book: _____

Author: _____

Did you like it?

_____
_____

Would you recommend it to others?

_____
_____

What impressed you most about this book?

_____
_____
_____
_____

How did God use the book to speak to you?

_____
_____
_____
_____

Other comments or thoughts about the book:

_____
_____
_____
_____

Lesson nine

VICTORY OVER SIN

Many Christians know that they love God but struggle constantly with sin. Different people have different areas of weakness and find that they keep stumbling at the same point. The Lord can deliver us and teach us to walk in victory.

WHAT IS SIN?

The literal Greek word for *sin* means "missing the mark," as illustrated by an arrow that doesn't hit its target. If our target is to please the Lord, we must learn how to have victory over sin. Sin is breaking God's laws. This includes doing what He tells us not to do (sins of commission) and failing to do what He tells us to do (sins of omission).

Romans 14:23b

_____

_____

James 4:17

_____

_____

The basis of sin is selfishness—a me-first attitude that can excuse any kind of behavior. If we picture sin as a tree, selfishness is the roots and the trunk. The branches and leaves on the tree are countless variations of self-will and rebellion.

THE PROBLEM OF ONGOING SIN

Struggling Christians who desperately want victory are very different from professing believers who are playing games with God. The first group of people are genuine children of God who are caught in a trap. They may weep and pray for freedom but don't know how to find it. They try hard to change but can't and thus feel overwhelmed. Reading the Bible is frightening because they constantly find verses relating to God's judgment of sin and His call to holiness. Defeated Christians can't seem to find the joy and peace God promises.

Romans 7:24

_____

_____

The second group are those who take the Lord very lightly. They count on a quick prayer to bring forgiveness for each sin but do not intend to leave those sins behind them.

Proverbs 28:13

_____

_____

The idea of offending and displeasing God doesn't concern this second group too much—these people just want to make it to heaven. Only God can see their hearts, but I am convinced that this kind of "believer" has never met Jesus.

1 John 3:6, 8 (*note that the Greek verb shows ongoing practice of sin*)

_____

_____

_____

Romans 2:4–5

_____

_____

_____

Galatians 6:7–8

_____

_____

_____

Titus 1:16

_____

_____

How Do We Deal with Sin?

Many Christians try to deal with the symptoms of sin instead of its cause. They think that working on an area of sin in their lives will fix it. This is like pruning a tree in the natural realm—it makes the tree stronger, and new branches grow to replace the ones that have been chopped off. Trying hard to meet God's requirements is not the way to victory.

1 Corinthians 15:56b

_____

_____

Galatians 3:3

_____

_____

God's intention for the laws of the Old Testament was to use them as a mirror to point out man's guilt. The Lord designed the sense of guilt that results from knowing the law and breaking it to make us humbly come to Jesus for forgiveness. He never meant the law to be the means of making us good enough for Him to accept us. Only grace, which means undeserved favor from God, can save us.

Ephesians 2:8–9

_____

_____

_____

_____

_____

1 Timothy 1:8–11

_____

_____

_____

_____

_____

Galatians 2:16

_____

_____

_____

_____

Galatians 3:19, 24

_____

_____

_____

_____

The way to deal with sin is not to put forth extra effort to perfect ourselves but to lay the ax to the root of the tree. This is repentance from sin itself, not just from individual sins.

Matthew 3:10

_____

_____

_____

TRUE STORY

While driving my car during a vacation one summer, I heard a preacher on a Christian station on my car radio. The preacher's simple challenge about sin has stuck with me ever since that day. The preacher asked his listeners, "If God gave you the choice to never sin again or to sin all you want and never have to worry about being judged for it, which would you choose? Your answer will tell you where your heart is." I thought about it and realized that I really want to please God. Fear of punishment isn't the key factor. The desire to never again sin is my heart's answer, although I'm tempted as often as you are. What would *your* answer be? What if the Lord appeared in the sky one day and announced that He was taking the weekend off with all the angels and no one would be keeping a record of what happened on earth. What do you think the world would be like?

God saw that the corruption of sin is so complete in the life of even a "good" person that there was no way to fix it. Selfishness has infected every bit of our lives.

Jeremiah 30:15

_____

_____

Romans 3:10–18

_____

_____

_____

_____

_____

The hopeless wickedness of humankind meant that our working on our weakness was not sufficient. Instead of giving us a repaired sinful life, God offers us a new life. This is not improvement; it is replacement.

2 Corinthians 5:17

_____

_____

This verse literally says that we become a new species of people. The Bible calls this the new man, and our life before we met Jesus is the old man.

Ephesians 4:22–24

_____

_____

_____

Colossians 3:9–10

_____

_____

_____

God tells us to take off the old man and put on the new man, just as we would change clothes. This is very different from the usual way Christians think about victory over sin. Trying to be a better Christian is like patching, washing, and ironing ugly, torn-up old clothes: no matter how much effort you put into it, you just don't have the basic stuff you need to work with. Wouldn't you rather get new clothes? If you got new clothes as a gift, wouldn't you want to go change out of your old clothes right away?

DEAD PEOPLE DON'T SIN

The way God exchanges our old life for a new life is through what Jesus accomplished on the cross. Jesus did more than pay for our sins on the cross, as wonderful as that is. He also destroyed the power of sin to rule over our lives. The sinful part of us was nailed to the cross with Him.

Romans 6:6–7

_____

_____

_____

Galatians 5:24

_____

_____

Galatians 2:20

_____

_____

Galatians 6:14

_____

_____

Colossians 3:3

_____

_____

If Jesus had died for our sins but had not broken the power of sin in our lives, we would end up right back in the same mess. Through the cross, Jesus removes the producer of sins—our old nature, or old self.

Now the old self is dead. Sometimes it doesn't seem like it, and we don't feel like it, but the Bible says it is so. Sin is not dead—it is very much alive all over the world. Your sinful *nature* is dead. God's nature in your life replaces your fallen nature. The commandments in the Bible take on a different light when you realize that it is your nature as a born-again Christian to obey them.

2 Peter 1:3–4

_____

_____

_____

Finding Victory over Temptation

"But I get tempted and fall so often!" Here's the key to getting out of that rut.

Romans 6:11–12

_____

_____

_____

The way we see our lives has a powerful effect.

Proverbs 23:7

_____

_____

We have the choice whether to let sin rule over us or reckon ourselves dead to sin. Here's how this works. Each of us is tempted in many ways every day. Being tempted is not a sign of sinfulness—even Jesus was tempted, yet He never sinned.

Matthew 4:1

_____

_____

Hebrews 4:15–16

_____

_____

_____

Many times, we feel guilty for being tempted, yet a temptation becomes a sin only when we agree to it by a choice of our will. Satan's strategy is to throw a fiery dart of temptation at us, then hit us with condemnation for being tempted. When you learn that temptation is an attack of the enemy and not a sign of being an evil person, you'll find much more freedom and peace in your walk with God.

1 John 3:21

_____

_____

Temptation is not a sign of weakness or lack of commitment to the Lord. As Paul did when the serpent attacked him on Malta, shake it off!

Acts 28:3–5

_____

_____

_____

You have no reason to repent for a temptation. You don't have to feel condemnation because of temptation. Here's how to respond when temptation hits—keep in mind that you're a dead man or woman. Dead people don't sin. You can curse at them, and they'll never get mad. You can hit them and not worry that they will hit back. Reckon or consider yourself to be dead to sin. Memorize and quote to yourself (or even out loud) the verses that make this clear. Say to yourself and to the devil, "The old me would have loved to do that, but he/she died on the cross with Jesus two thousand years ago. I'm a new creature now, and I'm free from the power of sin. I choose to serve the Lord!"

Your consistent choice to reaffirm obedience to the Lord breaks the habits of sin. You'll find increasing victory as you learn who you are in Jesus—a new creation! As the following verse states, we can choose what pleases Him.

Isaiah 56:4

_____

_____

This is the bottom line in victory over sin: the choice of our will to accept by faith what Jesus did on the cross for us. God gives us the freedom so that we can choose the right way, and He works in us so that we do choose the right way.

Philippians 2:13

_____

_____

_____

Notice in this verse that God is working on two areas: to will and to do. Once we will or choose to follow Him, He has no difficulty supplying the grace so that we can do it. A Christian with a total commitment to obey the Lord finds victory through the principles previously described. Let's never deceive ourselves into thinking that we somehow are destined to continually commit a particular sin. The reason some temptations are strong and constant is that we really want them. We put up a good fight, knowing all along that we'll give in later, but at least it looks good to the Lord. Yeah, right! If you have a sin problem, will you honestly ask the Lord if you're playing games with grace?

1 Corinthians 10:13

_____

_____

_____

2 Peter 2:9

_____

_____

_____

SIN, ORGANIZED CRIME, AND YOU

We're going to end this teaching with an illustration about new and old lives. You may have heard or seen on TV the way the government sometimes deals with criminals. When they catch a criminal who is a

TRUE STORY

Here's a disturbing thought: we have as much victory over sin as we want to have. The problem is in our will, not in a lack of power on God's part to help us not to sin. We make many excuses about why we do what we know we shouldn't do, but which sin have *you* ever committed in which you had no choice but to sin? Can you think of even one? No choice = no sin. There's always a choice. I'm seeing how accountable I am to the Lord for my actions. No excuse is big enough to hide behind. Since I can't keep any secrets from the Lord (Hebrews 4:13, Psalm 90:8), secret sin is really only a secret from other people, and God promises that those people will eventually find out (Numbers 32:23). I know that no matter how far I go in my ministry, status won't protect me from God's righteous judgments (1 Peter 4:17–18, Ezekiel 9:1–6). As a leader, I realize how widespread the consequences of a serious sin could be: many discouraged and wounded people, loss of respect from my own family, and hurting the ones I love the most. All these factors combine to keep me on track.

part of a network of other criminals, they may offer to let him turn state's evidence. This means that he will tell everything he knows about other criminals in exchange for either being freed from his own prison sentence or receiving a shorter prison term. This helps the law prosecute the major criminals who are the worst lawbreakers.

The problem with reporting other criminals is that this makes them angry and they may try to kill the informer. This is where a plan called the Federal Witness Protection Program goes into action. Since the former criminal who has helped the government is now in danger, the government finds him a new house, car, and job in another state. The government also gives him a new identity—a different name. The old man disappears forever: otherwise, the other criminals would find him and kill him. The person must receive a thorough change of identity to keep him safe from the old life. He doesn't have to invent the new identity. He's not told, "Do the best you can." It is part of the deal he receives for changing sides from crime to law and order. He receives not only pardon but also a new life because he changes sides. Pardon does not give him the freedom to turn in other criminals, leave prison, and go back to crime.

The person's part is to live out completely the new identity that the government has provided for him. He can't do it halfway—he can't sign his old name, answer to his old name, or hang around the places where he used to go as a criminal. Any of these things would put him in danger. He can't play the part as would an actor. An actor goes home after the performance and is really someone other than the character he or she plays. The former criminal must become the new man. He must break all associations with that old life and be the new man for the rest of his days.

After receiving pardon and receiving a new identity, the person should be very grateful. The government has forgiven his past, but if he foolishly commits new crimes, he will suffer the consequences. He has no immunity from the consequences of future crimes. He must not combine the old life with the new life. Now, as a new man, his slate is clean. He has a fresh start and a new identity, with the support of the most powerful organization in the country, the government.

Can you see the application to your own life? As a former criminal supplied with a new identity, don't go back to the old life! Learn not to respond when the enemy calls you by your old name. Realize, "That's not me anymore!" Live the rest of your life as a new person, with the support of the Lord Jesus Christ to help you. His grace and power are sufficient for you to live in a way that pleases the Lord.

Colossians 3:3–4

_____

_____

_____

APPLICATION

1. Think of the chief area of your life in which you struggle with sin. Can you relate that sin back to the root of selfishness?

2. Have you tried to deal with the symptoms of that sin or with its cause?

3. What does it mean for you to be a new creation in Jesus?

4. Do you ever feel guilty for being tempted? Has this teaching helped in that area?

FOLLOW-UP

1. Have you thought of your life differently this week, realizing that you are dead to sin?

2. Have you found more victory over sin this week?

3. Which Scripture verse helps you the most in realizing that God has provided you with victory over sin?

SCRIPTURE MEMORY

2 Corinthians 5:17–18 Therefore, if anyone is in Christ, he is a new creation; old things have passed away; behold, all things have become new. Now all things are of God, who has reconciled us to Himself through Jesus Christ, and has given us the ministry of reconciliation.

1 John 2:15–16 Do not love the world or the things in the world. If anyone loves the world, the love of the Father is not in him. For all that is in the world—the lust of the flesh, the lust of the eyes, and the pride of life—is not of the Father but is of the world.

DAILY BIBLE STUDY

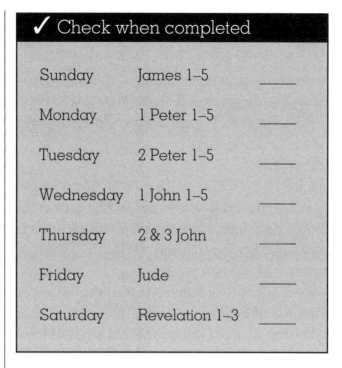

✓ Check when completed		
Sunday	James 1–5	_____
Monday	1 Peter 1–5	_____
Tuesday	2 Peter 1–5	_____
Wednesday	1 John 1–5	_____
Thursday	2 & 3 John	_____
Friday	Jude	_____
Saturday	Revelation 1–3	_____

BIBLE-READING QUESTIONS

_____
_____
_____
_____
_____
_____
_____
_____
_____
_____
_____

PRAYER NEEDS THIS WEEK

_____
_____
_____
_____
_____
_____
_____
_____
_____

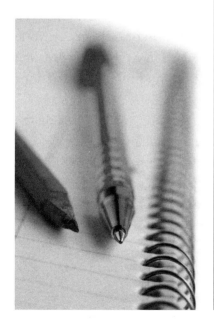

10

Lesson ten

Holiness

M any Christians misunderstand holiness. You'll see the word *holy* and its various forms approximately 640 times in the Bible, so this must be important to the Lord. Let's learn more about what holiness means and how to be holy.

What Holiness Isn't

Holiness is more than what we are on the outside. Many believers associate holiness with external things, like wearing only certain clothes and not playing cards or going to movies. It's easy to fall into the trap of legalism—believing that we can earn God's approval by following rules (both God's and our own) and thus make ourselves acceptable to Him. The result of legalism is self-righteousness and judging others.

God definitely wants our outside conduct to be right, but He wants righteous living to come from a pure heart. The real test of holiness is internal: What kind of person does God know us to be inside? What do we do when no one is looking? What kinds of thoughts do we have? What about our attitudes?

Psalm 51:6

_____

_____

What Holiness Is

Holiness means being set apart for a purpose. It is something that is separate, pure, and unmixed. Here are two examples from ordinary life that might help you understand the concept:

1. Some parking spaces are available for any car to park in them. Others are set apart for a specific purpose and marked by a sign so that everyone knows that they are not open to the public. The sign refers to who is allowed to use the spaces—handicapped people, the salesperson of the month at a store, the school principal, etc. When a Christian isn't holy, he or she is common or ordinary. Anyone or anything has access to his or her thoughts, motives, and life. Using the idea of a parking space, one time the city mayor parks there, another time a garbage truck uses it. It has no limits or restrictions placed on it.

2. Customers must call ahead to make reservations to eat at a fancy restaurant. A sign placed on the table shows that the table is reserved for the use of certain people and is not available to anyone else.

Holiness is like the sign on a parking space or on a table. It says that we are reserved for God's use and are available only to Him. In the Old Testament, the priests wore specific garments designed by God. Each garment had a symbolic meaning. On the front of their turbans the priests were to place a gold plaque that read, "Holiness to the Lord," showing that they were set apart for Him.

Exodus 28:36–38

_____

_____

This was a symbolic means of showing a spiritual truth: that they must be holy and that holiness must be visible in their lives for all to see. God called the priests to be noticeably different from those around them. An interesting example of this can be seen in the life of Elisha, who wasn't a priest and didn't wear a gold plaque.

2 Kings 4:8–9

_____

_____

_____

The Shunammite woman recognized Elisha as a holy man of God. There's no record of her having heard him preach or seen him do miracles. Maybe she had heard about his reputation, but she described him as being holy. Likewise, if we are holy men and women of God, people will hear about a difference in our lives and recognize that we are God's people. Don't go buy a turban and a gold plaque—instead live a holy life. The Lord calls all Christians to holiness.

1 Peter 1:15–16

_____

_____

_____

How Do We Become Holy?

Growing in holiness comes only by contact with the Lord, such as through worship, prayer, or studying the Word. It is not self-perfection.

2 Corinthians 3:17–18

_____

_____

_____

As we see the holiness of God and our own sinfulness by comparison, conviction strikes us. Every person in the Bible who encountered the Lord was awed (and terrified) by His Presence.

Isaiah 6:1–5

_____

_____

_____

_____

Job 40:3–4; 42:5–6

_____

_____

_____

_____

Compare this with Job's attitude in **Job 31:37**.

_____

_____

Matthew 17:5–6

_____

_____

_____

Luke 5:8

_____

_____

Our natural response to God's infinite power and holiness would be to flee from Him, yet in His presence, we can sense His mercy and love. We remain before Him in worship or prayer, and the work of God's grace changes us into His image. God slays some areas of sin in a moment, while others require the ongoing work of the Holy Spirit. Seeing His holiness changes our hearts—the evil things we once loved become disgusting to us in His light.

Isaiah 30:22

_____

_____

We grow in holiness as we set our lives apart to serve Jesus. Increasing love for the Lord and desire to please Him will cause us to separate ourselves from the things that offend Him, and we'll become holy without legalistic or self-righteous attitudes.

We must realize how serious holiness is. This is not an elective course but a requirement for every Christian. Sometimes the lack of emphasis on holiness in most preaching and teaching makes people think that holiness is just for ultradedicated Christians, those who want to go above and beyond the call of duty, but Scripture shows this to be a deception. Let the weight of the following verse cause you to think.

Hebrews 12:14

_____

_____

The reason that unbelievers take God lightly is that they have no understanding of His otherness. God is utterly different from fallen man in this area as well as in many other facets of His nature. Is it possible that many Christians also think that God is like them, in their imperfect and unholy condition? Keep in mind that God calls us to be holy as He is holy.

Psalm 50:21

_____

_____

_____

_____

Our Standard of Holiness

Sometimes we feel that we are great Christians because we have certain parts of our lives worked out more than other Christians do. Even if this were true, it doesn't mean that we are holy in God's sight; it means only that we are holier than the person we are judging. Can you see how pride and self-righteousness enter into such a situation? We may believe that we are holy because we are different from unsaved people. Neither of these comparisons is valid. Scripture says that using another person as the standard of comparison is foolish.

2 Corinthians 10:12

_____

_____

_____

_____

Our standard of holiness is the Lord Jesus Christ. Only in His life will we find an unchanging example of holiness both internally and externally.

Hebrews 13:8

_____

_____

_____

_____

Malachi 3:6

_____

_____

TRUE STORY

Sometimes I cringe, and it's not just at the jokes non-Christians tell. Have you ever heard believers tell a joke that takes God lightly? Maybe one that makes Him seem a little more human than divine—flawed like us? Maybe you've heard a flippant prayer that obviously wasn't directed toward the Lord but was designed to get people to laugh. It's not that God doesn't have a sense of humor. But He is still God, and He is holy. By linking Him with sin in a joke, we show a lack of respect or reverence, which Scripture refers to as the fear of the Lord. The world around us has lost the fear of the Lord and mixes the holy and the unholy in the same breath. Have you ever heard food described as sinfully delicious or so good it must be a sin (Proverbs 14:9)? And what about the flippant way even many Christians use God's Name? I'm careful not even to say "Oh, my God!"

The world is far worse. Once I was waiting in line to pick up my food at a taco restaurant when the man in front of me discovered that his order had been misplaced. The man ranted and raved at the cashier, using every swear word I've ever heard. The tacos at that restaurant aren't even that good—definitely not worth this level of tantrum. When the man ran out of profanity, he turned to blasphemy, spitting out the words, "Jesus Christ!" All this over missing tacos! I immediately tapped him on the shoulder. The man turned around, his face contorted with rage, and I looked him in the eye and said, "He's Lord, you know." The man fished for something to say, couldn't come up with a reply, and silently turned back to the cowering cashier. I've stopped people in many settings who were using God's Name this way.

The world's standard of right and wrong is constantly changing—usually going downhill except in times of spiritual awakening that bring the fear of God on unbelievers.

2 Timothy 3:13

_____

_____

When Christians allow their standard of holiness to be anything less than Jesus Himself, they slowly follow the downward spiral of the world. They end up in the same sins the world loves, just a little behind it. The Church has accepted much of the world's sin today as a result of a slow erosion of holiness. For example, divorce is a sad fact even in Christian marriages. The divorce rate among Christians is nearly as high as it is among unbelievers. Few churches take a stand against divorce with the intensity that reflects God's feelings about it.

Malachi 2:16

_____

_____

_____

Abortion is still unacceptable to most believers, but doctors in the United States perform one out of every six abortions on self-described evangelical Christian women—150,000 per year. What does the Lord think about this?

Proverbs 6:16–19

_____

_____

_____

_____

Now some professing Christians argue for the acceptance of homosexuality. The liberal perspective on the gay lifestyle is that we should accept people as they are, not make people feel bad about themselves, not judge them, but simply love them. Some claim that culture has changed since Bible days and that certain verses are no longer relevant. In an effort to love the sinner, we have accepted the sin. Jesus calls us to judge situations and people righteously, which means according to God's standards. This is very different from the prideful human tendency to criticize or put others down to build themselves up. Righteous judgment is a responsibility of the Church.

Romans 1:24–28

_____

_____

_____

_____

John 7:24

_____

_____

1 Corinthians 5:11–6:3

_____

_____

_____

_____

Satan's Strategy to Destroy Holiness

When it suits his purposes, the devil can be very patient. Since he knows that it would be too difficult to bring a Christian down from a holy life to deep sin in a brief amount of time, his strategy is slow and steady pressure.

Daniel 7:25 *(The literal Hebrew word for* persecute *here means to wear out.)*

_____

_____

Satan's first step is to get our eyes off Jesus as our standard of holiness. Once we have lost Him as our fixed and unchanging standard, deception can gradually set in. Temptations come for us to move just a little step in the direction of the world. All the while, the world's standard is also moving. Once we have taken the first small step, the next temptation calls us to take another small step. The voice of temptation says, "It isn't that bad, compared to where you are now." Unless God is able to get our attention, we forget that where we are now is already sin.

Little by little, sin ensnares us as we fail to realize that we are now doing things that would have horrified us earlier in our walk with God. Since the world is going deeper into sin, and we've kept the gap constant between us and the world, we are deceived into believing we're okay. The voice of our conscience is easy to ignore—we can turn down the volume of the Holy Spirit's voice by hardening our hearts.

The sad problem of sexual sin among Christian students is the best illustration of this satanic strategy. Very few young people who love the Lord would jump right into a temptation to commit fornication, but by taking each small step in that direction, young people can end up in very serious sin. At any point along the way they could look to Jesus and recognize how far they have already fallen. It's unfortunate that many Christians don't realize what's going on until they are jolted back to reality once the fall has taken place.

Ephesians 4:27

_____

_____

1 Peter 2:11

_____

_____

A famous non-Christian comedienne once gave an example of the way the world's standard changes. She said that when she tries out a new joke, if people gasp rather than laugh, she puts away the joke for six months. "Then when I try the joke again," she continued, "the audience will laugh." She didn't know that a biblical principle was at work: things that people refuse to accept today won't seem so bad in six months in the eyes of a lost world. How sad that the Church often falls into the trap that is destroying the unsaved.

Practical Steps to Holiness

We must take to heart God's call to be holy. We have a responsibility to make changes in our lives based on the grace He provides for us.

2 Corinthians 7:1

_____

_____

1 John 3:3

_____

_____

Deuteronomy 23:14

_____

_____

In a world so full of uncleanness and lust, the area of sexual sin and immorality is one of the major temptations young believers face.

2 Peter 1:3–4

_____

_____

The Bible gives us, in addition to the steps explained in the "Victory over Sin" teaching, a key to living in holiness. Always be careful of what you allow to come into your life, especially through your eyes. Our hearts follow what our eyes see. Once we have let evil influences enter through our eyes, we're tempted to let them take root inside our hearts and minds.

Psalm 101:3

_____

_____

Job 31:1

_____

_____

Job 31:7

_____

_____

Lamentations 3:51 *(If available, read the King James Version.)*

_____

_____

Jeremiah 4:14

_____

_____

Isaiah 55:7

_____

_____

When we face temptations to commit physical sin, we're more likely to fall if mental sin has weakened our defenses. It's easy to do something in your body if you've rehearsed it a thousand times in your mind. This is why Scripture tells us to guard our hearts and our minds carefully.

Proverbs 4:23

_____

_____

You don't have to go with the flow and follow either the world or Christian friends who don't live according to God's standard of holiness. It isn't easy to face rejection or ridicule that will probably come your way if you live God's way. Sometimes you'll feel like you're the only one who cares about doing right, but you're not alone.

Romans 11:2–5

_____

_____

_____

If you can demonstrate holiness with humility, the Holy Spirit will convict people around you. Just don't let a self-righteous attitude develop in your life. Be an example of genuine Christianity for both the saved and the lost people around you to follow.

Application

1. When was the last time you tried to act or look holy?

2. Have you ever tried to become more holy? Did it work?

3. Have you ever compared yourself to others instead of Jesus?

4. What does it mean for your life to be set apart for the Lord?

Follow-Up

1. How have you felt pressure from the enemy to move away from God's standard of holiness?

2. When was the last time you were tempted to allow unholy things to come into your life through your eyes?

3. In a world that is growing more evil all the time, how will you keep God's standard of holiness?

SCRIPTURE MEMORY

2 Corinthians 7:1 Therefore, having these promises, beloved, let us cleanse ourselves from all filthiness of the flesh and spirit, perfecting holiness in the fear of God.

1 Peter 1:15–16 [B]ut as He who called you is holy, you also be holy in all your conduct, because it is written, "Be holy, for I am holy."

DAILY BIBLE STUDY

✓ Check when completed

Sunday	Revelation 4–6	_____
Monday	Revelation 7–9	_____
Tuesday	Revelation 10–13	_____
Wednesday	Revelation 14–16	_____
Thursday	Revelation 17–19	_____
Friday	Revelation 20–22	_____
Saturday	*Congratulations—you did it!*	

BIBLE-READING QUESTIONS

_____
_____
_____
_____
_____
_____
_____
_____
_____

PRAYER NEEDS THIS WEEK

_____
_____
_____
_____
_____
_____
_____
_____
_____

11

Lesson eleven

BEING AN EXAMPLE

The biggest charge against Christianity from unbelievers is that Christians are hypocrites. This isn't true for many genuine believers, but the lost often use this as an excuse. They hold us to a standard of righteousness that they don't themselves hold, but usually it is a right standard. They charge us with hypocrisy when they see a Christian who isn't like Jesus, and sometimes they are right. Devastating, isn't it?

THE PROBLEM OF HYPOCRISY

Jesus was called a friend of sinners (Matthew 11:19). He showed compassion to people who were humble and repentant, no matter how awful their sins were (Luke 7:36–50), but His harshest words were reserved for hypocrites.

Matthew 23:13

_____

_____

We usually recognize hypocrisy in others but not in ourselves. Until God's work of brokenness and humility takes effect in our lives, it's easy to deceive ourselves and judge others.

God still hates hypocrisy. He wants reality and genuineness in our lives.

Psalm 51:6

_____

_____

John 14:17

_____

_____

Truth pleases God, but anything fake displeases Him (Deuteronomy 25:13–16; Revelation 21:27). He wants our lives to be the same on the inside as they are on the outside. It's like furniture: some pieces are made of solid, quality wood, while others are made of cheap materials covered by a thin coating of fine wood called veneer. Too many people look good on the outside, but God knows their hearts. We have many veneer Christians today.

Matthew 23:27

_____

_____

Hypocrites are like a fake building at Universal Studios. From one angle the building looks real, but as you go around the side, you see it's only a front propped up by beams behind it. Many people put up a front to impress others, but it's hard to keep up a false impression. The lies propping up a false front are unstable, and other people usually discover the truth.

THE CONSEQUENCES OF HYPOCRISY

Hypocrisy is a stumbling block that can keep people from coming to Jesus. We don't know the consequences of our lives while we're still on earth. We're either positively or negatively affecting people we live with, work with, and go to school with. The consequences of those people's choice to serve the Lord or reject Him can be enormous.

Mohandas Gandhi spent time with evangelical Christians in Africa and England. He heard the gospel and was familiar with Christianity before he returned to India and led that vast group of people. Gandhi later wrote, "I would be convinced to become a Christian if it were not for the Christians." In other words, he believed that Christianity might be true, but he saw the lives of Christians falling short of the faith they professed. He remained a Hindu, and his nation remains in darkness.

Karl Marx also heard the gospel. His sister-in-law was a Christian, and he lived in Germany and London during a time of revival. Three of his children died of malnutrition, and he developed great bitterness toward Christians. He considered Christians to be hypocrites, and rather than embrace Christianity, he developed the man-centered theology of communism.

Together these two men affected the lives of more than half the population of the world. What might the world be like if Gandhi had returned to India as a believer and had led his country to Jesus? Or if Marx had put his efforts into the kingdom of God?

We don't know who is watching our lives now or how we might change the world by living a truly godly life and showing God's light to others.

THE POWER OF TRUE CHRISTIANITY

There's something so marvelous about genuine Christians. People recognize a quality that's different

TRUE STORY

I once saw an incredible example of hypocrisy and judgment. A Christian young man came one time in a rage to see me. His father was the pastor of a church in our city. "My dad is such a hypocrite! That fake! That phony!" the young man fumed. This made me curious, and I asked him what was going on. He explained that he (the pastor's son) had been looking in the TV guide and had seen that a program called America's Greatest Strippers was scheduled on cable TV in the middle of the night. He had set his alarm to get up and watch the program. "But when I got up, my dad was already in there watching it! And he calls himself a Christian! That hypocrite!"

I was stunned and I asked him, "What about you? You were going in there to watch the same program."

He responded, "That's not the point. The point is my father—the phony."

"But you planned to commit the same sin."

"Yeah, well, that was wrong, but my dad…"

I couldn't convince the young man to let go of his judgmental, hypocritical attitude and repent of his own sin. He had a bad case of spiritual blindness.

about them. When a person is a true example of the Lord, God's Presence convicts sinners and draws the empty and the hurting. Christians' good works bring glory to God and silence His enemies.

Matthew 5:16

_____

_____

Titus 2:7–8

_____

_____

_____

When a person claims to be a Christian but doesn't live like a follower of Jesus Christ, the opposite takes place.

Titus 1:16

_____

_____

Romans 2:23–24

_____

_____

_____

If we will live out our faith, we will change the lives and destinies of people around us because God's Spirit will flow through us. Many Christians don't understand how to have the flow of the Holy Spirit in their lives. They feel as though God uses only superspiritual people, but God doesn't play favorites.

Romans 2:11

_____

_____

God will use everyone who has truly submitted his or her will to Him. It doesn't work to walk in the flesh and then try to turn on the Holy Spirit. If you're walking in the Spirit (Galatians 5:25), you can be a vessel of God's power. To live casually and selfishly and then to expect a quick prayer to qualify you to be useful to God is an abuse of grace. No power or anointing is available cheaply.

On rare occasions, the Lord may allow His anointing to flow through a believer who has turned away from Him—or even through an unbeliever. This works when the person is in an office or a position that God has ordained. King Saul prophesied after he had fallen into sin (1 Samuel 19:23–24). As the high priest, Caiaphas prophesied Jesus' death, then plotted to crucify Jesus (John 11:49–53).

LIVING LIKE JESUS

Sometimes Christians say, "Don't look at me, look at Jesus." This is partly true—people shouldn't look to us to solve their problems, and we shouldn't receive glory when God uses us. Yet when people look at us, they should see Jesus in us.

1 John 4:17

_____

_____

_____

If people can't look at us and see Him, we're not living "as He is." The apostle Paul made many startling claims to being "as He is." Let's look at some of them.

Philippians 4:9

_____

_____

_____

Note that Paul said, "Not just what you learned and heard, but what you saw in me."

1 Corinthians 11:1

_____

_____

_____

1 Corinthians 4:15–16

_____

_____

_____

_____

Philippians 3:17

_____

_____

_____

Paul was confident that his life was an example of everything he preached.

2 Timothy 3:10–11

_____

_____

TRUE STORY

Her dad was a preacher, but that didn't stop her. At fifteen, Maria went over the edge to years of an outrageously promiscuous lifestyle and drug use. Her brokenhearted parents tried to reason with her when she ran away to live with a satanist. But Maria told them that they had had *their* fun before they came to the Lord, and she planned to do the same. I couldn't get through to her, either, and Maria left the youth group.

One of the youth group girls had overheard a conversation in a classroom about sex. As the others discussed immoral kids, the worst example they could think of was Maria. One girl, when some members of our group from Maria's school were witnessing and inviting people to our meetings, replied fiercely, "I know someone from your group— Maria—and if you're anything like her, I don't want to have anything to do with you!" Maria eventually came back home, but she had dragged Jesus' Name and reputation through the filth of her life. How much damage had she done to the kingdom?

TRUE STORY

My wife and I take teenagers and college students on mission outreaches all over the world. Our life is exciting and challenging as we go to Asia, South America, and Africa for up to five weeks at a time. I realized early on that the real person comes out on a trip during which thirty-five people live in close quarters, facing stressful living conditions and spiritual warfare together. There's no way to hide anything. The group would come away with either more respect for my walk with God or none at all. Would my conduct inspire or disappoint the youth who look up to me? So much rides on the outcome of this test.

By the mercy of God—and I don't have any delusions about having perfect Christian character—it has worked out well. Many times both kids and staff have marveled at my patience, which is funny to me because I know myself to be an inwardly impatient person. It's the fruit of the Holy Spirit to show self-control that saves the day, and I'm usually at least outwardly patient.

The other aspect that makes a big difference in the outcome is that I make it a priority to ask forgiveness as publicly as I blow it, which still happens all too often. I'll stand before the group several times during the course of a trip and apologize to Melissa for snapping at her or to Frank for barking orders in a busy situation. Let's be sure to give our leaders the right to still be human beings. That is mercy, and I know *I* need it.

1 Thessalonians 1:5–6

_____

_____

_____

_____

1 Thessalonians 2:8, 10

_____

_____

_____

_____

Paul claimed that even God was a witness of the genuine example of his life.

2 Thessalonians 3:7, 9

_____

_____

_____

_____

God has given us spiritual leaders as examples, and He calls us to follow them. If you respect your pastor or youth leader, you'll learn from their sermons. If your leader is a person of genuine integrity, you'll learn even more by watching his or her life. Ask for opportunities to walk through daily life with your leader. See how he or she treats others: his or her spouse and children, his or her followers, waiters at a restaurant, and any others he or she comes into contact with. This will tell you more about a person than a well-planned Bible study or sermon. See whether your leader looks for and recognizes opportunities to share the gospel, shows patience while driving and waiting in line, tells appropriate jokes, serves others, walks in humility, admits to wrongs, and honors God in every aspect of life. This is not a suggestion for you to give your leaders a report card or wait for them to blow it. Recognize that everyone falls short in many respects (James 3:2). Rather, this is an opportunity for you to see how the principles of walking with God work out in real life.

Hebrews 6:12

_____

_____

Hebrews 13:17

_____

_____

We are spiritual examples to others. Our godly lifestyle can inspire anyone who looks up to us, or our failures can cause others to stumble. Responsibility and grace go together as we seek to be as Jesus is in this world. Don't feel you can't live up to this—let God's grace change your life so that you can help change the world. You can be a blameless and upright example for others to follow.

Psalm 37:37

_____

_____

APPLICATION

1. Give an example of hypocrisy you have witnessed. Have you forgiven that person if his or her failure wounded you?

2. Have you ever realized the power of your example to influence others?

3. Can you say what Paul said in Philippians 4:9? Why or why not?

FOLLOW-UP

1. Who has watched the example of your life this week?

2. How has your example this week influenced someone else to live for the Lord?

3. Name someone you see regularly whom you would like to influence for the Lord. How can you be an example to that person?

SCRIPTURE MEMORY

Matthew 28:18–20 And Jesus came and spoke to them, saying, "All authority has been given to Me in heaven and on earth. Go therefore and make disciples of all the nations, baptizing them in the name of the Father and of the Son and of the Holy Spirit, teaching them to observe all things that I have commanded you; and lo, I am with you always, even to the end of the age." Amen.

FILL OUT SPIRITUAL GROWTH QUESTIONNAIRE 2 ON THE NEXT PAGE.

FILL OUT AND SEND IN THE COURSE EVALUATION ON PAGES 155–156.

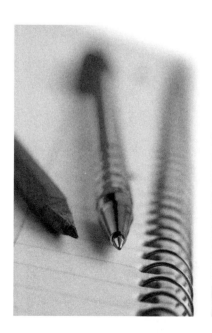

DAILY BIBLE STUDY

✓ Check when completed

Sunday

Monday

Tuesday

Wednesday

Thursday

Friday

Saturday

(Use this week to catch up if you're behind schedule. Or begin rereading the New Testament or start reading the Old Testament.)

BIBLE-READING QUESTIONS

_____
_____
_____
_____
_____
_____
_____
_____
_____

PRAYER NEEDS THIS WEEK

_____
_____
_____
_____
_____
_____
_____
_____
_____

12

Spiritual Growth Questionnaire 2

1. My relationship with the Lord is

(distant)   1   2   3   4   5   6   7   8   9   10   (intimate)

2. My knowledge of the Bible is

(very little)   1   2   3   4   5   6   7   8   9   10   (very much)

3. My Bible reading is

(inconsistent) 1   2   3   4   5   6   7   8   9   10   (steady)

4. My awareness of missions is

(very little)   1   2   3   4   5   6   7   8   9   10   (very much)

5. My understanding of God's plan for my life is

(very little)   1   2   3   4   5   6   7   8   9   10   (very much)

6. My prayer life is

(nonexistent) 1   2   3   4   5   6   7   8   9   10   (powerful)

ADDITIONAL COMMENTS FOR YOURSELF (OPTIONAL):

_____

_____

_____

_____

_____

_____

_____

_____

Now compare these answers to your answers on the Spiritual Growth Questionnaire 1 on page 30.

Lesson twelve

How to Keep Growing Spiritually

A major problem in the lives of many Christians is becoming stagnant in their walk with God. Obvious sin might not have snared them, but the zeal and enthusiasm for God that they once had are gone, and they stop growing in the Lord. Stagnancy begins once complacency has set in: people lose interest in the things of God and become spiritually bored. Eventually they find themselves wrapped up more and more in the things of the world, and they become stagnant.

Sinking Slowly

Stagnant Christians have begun to seek what the Gentiles seek rather than the kingdom of God (Matthew 6:32–33). They then lose their sensitivity to the voice of the Holy Spirit and begin to sink slowly into spiritual quicksand. Subtle heart and mind changes take place. On the outside, things might look all right, since no sin is obvious, but the person's spiritual life has become just a shell, with no life inside. Finally, many end up leaving their first love.real

Revelation 2:4

_____

_____

Notice that Jesus doesn't say that they have *lost* their first love, like a misplaced treasure they would search for until it's found (Luke 15:8–9). He says that they have *left* their first love. This shows a conscious choice to place other things as the main focus of their lives, which is the place only Jesus deserves to fill. God's Word warns us about this trap and how it can develop.

Colossians 3:1–2

_____

_____

_____

Luke 21:34

_____

_____

Matthew 13:22

_____

_____

The sad thing is that these believers may continue to go through the religious motions of regularly attending church, being good, moral people, and tithing, but they have lost the realness of the relationship with God that they once had.

Romans 12:11

_____

_____

Jeremiah 2:13

_____

_____

In the preceding verse, God describes Himself as the Fountain of Living Waters. He is the source of a continually fresh flow of spiritual life, but He says that His people turn away from Him and store water in a tank called a cistern. This water starts out fresh but quickly becomes stagnant. Bugs and algae make it unfit to drink, and a cistern has no source within it to replenish it. This is a close parallel to the lives of many believers who try to replenish the blessings of God as they live from one spiritual high to the next. You probably know Christians who desperately look forward to the next camp, retreat, conference, or spiritual fix to boost their waning walk with the Lord. How very sad this is, when just staying in tune with the Lord would provide continual refreshing.

Even sadder is that this level of spiritual life is all that many churches expect—being faithful in attendance, giving regularly, and living a clean life. However, these outside actions are no substitute for a heart right with God. Even living this way with a pure heart is only the starting point of a Christian's life.

We want to help you avoid becoming a mediocre Christian and keep the fire going inside. We don't want you to go from being a zealous and enthusiastic young believer to an adult in a spiritual rut, stuck in a comfortable nine-to-five routine, wrapped up in materialism, and missing the plan of God for your life. Because the Father is glorified by our bearing much fruit (John 15:8), we want to see you become a hundredfold Christian, not a thirtyfold or a sixtyfold one. Here are some ideas about how to avoid the trap of becoming a joyless Christian slug, useless to the kingdom and missing the adventure of walking with Jesus.

Keys to Keeping Your Spiritual Fire Burning
Seek out fellowship with people who are more spiritually mature than you are.

Proverbs 13:20

_____

_____

You will usually become like the people you spend the most time with. It's not that these people have to teach you anything formally, but you'll absorb their lives and lifestyle into your own life. This can be either good or bad, depending on the kind of people you choose to spend your time with.

Proverbs 12:26

_____

_____

1 Corinthians 15:33

_____

_____

God doesn't want us to stay away from unsaved people. Jesus was called a friend of sinners (Matthew 11:19), and we need to have relationships with lost people to love them and point them to the Lord. The big question is, Who is influencing whom? Who leads the friendship? Who chooses where to go and what to do? Remember to avoid covenants with unsaved people. This means relationships in which you are yoked or joined by promises and commitments, especially in dating and marriage.

2 Corinthians 6:14–18

_____

_____

_____

_____

It doesn't take much to dull the cutting edge of an ax (Ecclesiastes 10:10). To be a tool of the Lord, you must be in good spiritual shape. After all the effort you've put into sharpening your spiritual life during IDC, don't let ungodly friends pull you down. Spend time regularly with people who are an example to you of how to live a Christian life. Seek out those you admire as genuine men and women of God. If you and your mentor have developed a close relationship, why not ask if you could continue to be accountable to him or her and still meet for prayer?

Seek out spiritual input that shows that you haven't made it yet. Challenging messages will take you beyond spiritual maintenance into continuing progress in the Lord. These will often be disturbing messages—calls to dedication, holiness, sacrifice, burden for the lost, even martyrdom. Cutting-edge messages use the sword of the Spirit, the Word of God, to reveal truth you're not yet living in. You may feel some discomfort as men and women of God call you out of your comfort zone, but each of us needs some messages that make us say "Amen" and some that make us say "Ouch!" This is not a suggestion for you to look into questionable sources or bad doctrine.

Hebrews 13:9

_____

_____

Matthew 16:6

_____

_____

Never read cult materials such as the Book of Mormon or the Koran unless God specifically directs you to them (for example, if you are witnessing to a cult member) and your spiritual leaders know about it. False doctrine carries a counterfeit spiritual power, a type of demonic anointing to deceive.

1 Timothy 4:1

_____

_____

Galatians 1:6–9

_____

_____

_____

The kind of teaching we need in order to grow contains more than just facts and ideas. It comprises messages that cause us to lose interest in worldly things, to search the Scriptures, and to lie awake at night praying. For God to do deep work in our lives He must cut deeply to bring evil to light and cleanse us from it. It's a good thing to realize, "I have so far to go!" A hard message, preached under the leading of the Holy Spirit, will always point to the grace of God rather than to human effort to change. The enemy may try to use strong messages against us through hopelessness or guilt, but in the end, a person genuinely seeking God will benefit. God will apply His truth in the proper way.

Hebrews 12:5–11

_____

_____

_____

_____

We must never abort the work of the Holy Spirit in our lives by avoiding the truth. Don't throw out conviction by confusing it with condemnation. Many Christians avoid disturbing messages because of the "let's-feel-good-about-ourselves" mentality that the Church has absorbed from the world. The messages our flesh avoids are the ones we need the most.

Psalm 85:8

_____

_____

Let's be like Jacob, who wrestled with the angel all night and came away limping but transformed (Genesis 32:24–32). There are times when we wrestle over points of truth that we would rather not hear or over calls from the Lord that will take our lives in a new direction. Once we have been through a time like Jacob went through, we will find our character changed.

Watch your diet. Spiritually speaking, of course. We all need a balance in the amount and kind of food we eat. Athletes training for the Olympics need more than the USRDA to perform their best, and they know that a few extra donuts here and there could keep them from a gold medal. When they are working out and burning many calories, they need vitamins and extra amounts of good food. In the same way, a Christian who wants to be in the middle of what God is doing must be careful to avoid ungodly things and to take in extra helpings from God's table.

1 Corinthians 10:21

A sermon or two a week isn't enough spiritual food, but that's all that many Christians want. Because pastors and other spiritual leaders must aim at the middle level of spiritual maturity in the congregation, a growing believer will need more meat than a Sunday service alone can usually provide. If your leader offers special classes or Bible studies, attend them. Absorb all you can from the man or woman of God who is your spiritual covering.

Learn to feed yourself. It's fine for a baby bird to sit in the nest with its mouth open, waiting for its mother to drop food into it. As the bird grows, it must go looking for its own food. You must eventually learn to feed yourself spiritually. First, you will want to determine which spiritual diet you want to follow. You'll find that every spiritual leader has a particular emphasis or message. One concentrates on prayer, another emphasizes evangelism, a third, social action.

To round out your spiritual diet, find men and women of God with revelation from God in different areas. I learned a great deal by seeking God's truth in this way. From one pastor I learned what it means to be in Christ; from another, what it's like to have a burden for souls. One evangelist has an emphasis on holiness, another on prayer, others on the anointing and miracles. From a missionary I saw firsthand what our mission is and how to live in faithfulness to that call. Leaders who have a life message in each area are the best teachers.

Put into practice what you're learning. What you learn mentally but don't practice is like spiritual fat instead of muscle. If God has given you revelation of Himself and His truth, live it and give it to others. This way you'll make room for more growth in your own life as well as help others grow.

James 1:22–25

TRUE STORY

I know several Christian leaders whom I am always eager to see. It may be the chance to go out for lunch or coffee or just to meet to work on some ministry business, but I feel spiritually refreshed after talking with them. This takes place because I respect these men and women of God and see in them a genuine walk with the Lord. These leaders may not pass on gems of spiritual truth or deep revelations of the kingdom, but I absorb some of the life they are giving off. I leave these meetings humbled and desirous of drawing closer to the Lord and living a more holy life than before. The dedication and sacrifices of these leaders cause me to lay down my life more for the kingdom. I hope that *my* life has this effect on others.

1 Corinthians 8:1

_____

_____

Israel has two large bodies of water. The Sea of Galilee is full of fish and other life, while the Dead Sea is, well, dead. Nothing can live in the Dead Sea. The difference between the two bodies of water is that the Sea of Galilee has input from various rivers, then output into the Jordan River, and it never becomes stagnant. The Dead Sea, on the other hand, only receives water and doesn't give any out, and it is lifeless.

If we fail to give out what the Lord has given to us, we'll miss one of the crucial keys to personal spiritual growth and keep others from receiving God's blessings. We have a responsibility both to the Lord and to people around us to pass it on.

Luke 12:48

_____

_____

2 Timothy 2:2

_____

_____

Be faithful to spiritual disciplines. The habits IDC required will help you all through your life if you'll continue them. You've been studying Scripture, praying, tithing, learning responsibility, being concerned for the lost, and avoiding worldly influences. The tendency is to coast on the growth you've experienced. Don't do it! Press on into all God has for you.

Philippians 3:12–14

_____

_____

_____

Cultivate a heart that seeks after God—the real key to continued growth. Do you have a cry in your heart for God—not just a prayer but a deep desperation to know Him more, walk closely with Him, and please Him each day? Scripture shows this longing, which is still found in the hearts of disciples.

Psalm 27:8

_____

_____

Psalm 42:1–2

_____

_____

_____

Psalm 84:1–2, 10

_____

_____

_____

_____

If you want to avoid backsliding or becoming a mediocre and fruitless Christian, adopt one simple rule for your life: seek the Lord and obey what He says.

Hebrews 3:7–8

_____

_____

_____

_____

Choose a spiritual leader and/or church community carefully. Avoid a church where the message is "Just come, sit, and tithe." Don't attend a church with comforting and soft messages that promote worldly values. Beware of "self" ministry: be all you can be, with an emphasis on wealth, success, and reaching your potential. This is humanism, no matter how many Bible verses such ministries distort to support their teachings. Watch out for glamorous and flashy ministries. They are usually fleshly. God is awesome, and you'll sense humility and brokenness in His true servants. Just as in the days of the Old Testament, God does not want flesh showing in His Presence (Exodus 20:26).

Even large and well-known ministries may not be pleasing to the Lord if their focus is on man instead of God. Keep in mind that it's not our place to judge them, but we must look at their fruit. It's not the size of a ministry but the kind of ministry that's important to God (1 Corinthians 3:13). Heaven will reveal some surprises when rewards are distributed.

Matthew 19:30

TRUE STORY

Recently I felt an uncomfortable distance growing in my walk with the Lord. Perhaps you've experienced the same thing in a friendship or with a family member: a sense of awkwardness, an undercurrent of tension, just not clicking as you once did. Maybe you didn't even have a clue about what was wrong, but finally you asked, "What did I do?" When I asked the Lord this question, His reply brought a sense of conviction that my attitudes toward others weren't right. Instances immediately came to my mind—criticizing, judging, gossiping, making cynical comments to be funny. In each instance, God had shown His disapproval before I had ever actually made the comments. But I had ignored His warning and sinned in my words, because I had already sinned in my heart. I saw that some anger and frustration that I had failed to take to the cross was the root of the problem. When I humbled my heart and sincerely asked for forgiveness, the cloud lifted right away and I felt peace again. Let's be careful not to let sin stack up in our lives.

_____

_____

True ministry will fulfill the purposes God has shown in His Word. People will hear God's call to come out from the wickedness of this world and serve the Lord in holiness.

Ezekiel 22:26

_____

_____

Ezekiel 44:23

_____

_____

Jeremiah 23:21–22

_____

_____

_____

Attend church. Be sure to stay connected to a church at all times in your Christian life. It's too easy to make excuses and have a critical spirit toward churches, but this is a deadly mistake. Go to church!

Hebrews 10:25

_____

_____

You can have a dynamic Christian life from now until you see the Lord face-to-face. There's no need for your zeal to cool off or your heart to become cold. Press on to follow Jesus!

Application

1. Have you gone through times of spiritual growth followed by times of complacency and stagnancy?

2. Why or why not?

3. Which of the keys to keeping your spiritual fire burning will help you to continue growing spiritually?

Follow-Up

1. What steps will you take to continue to grow spiritually after IDC ends?

    a.

    b.

    c.

    d.

2. How can you give to others what God has taught you in IDC?

    a.

    b.

    c.

    d.

RESOURCES

YOU'VE FINISHED twelve weeks of challenge. Here are some resources to help you continue growing and learning. Don't stop challenging yourself!

My New Identity

I AM the righteousness of God in Christ. (2 Corinthians 5:21)

I CAN do all things through Christ who strengthens me. (Philippians 4:13)

I AM free from the power of sin. (Romans 6:6–14)

I AM a new creation in Christ—old things have passed away, and all things have become new. (2 Corinthians 5:17)

"Those who are Christ's have crucified the flesh with its passions and desires." (Galatians 5:24)

"I have been crucified with Christ; it is no longer I who live, but Christ lives in me; and the life which I now live in the flesh I live by faith in the Son of God, who loved me and gave Himself for me." (Galatians 2:20)

"Then I will give them one heart, and I will put a new spirit within them, and take the stony heart out of their flesh, and give them a heart of flesh, that they may walk in My statutes and keep My judgments and do them; and they shall be My people, and I will be their God." (Ezekiel 11:19–20)

The old me...	The new me...
pouted and felt sorry for myself	refuses to live selfishly (Matthew 16:24)
hated others	loves others (1 John 4:7–11)
was greedy	gives freely (Luke 6:38; Matthew 10:8)
delighted in sin	delights in obeying God (Romans 7:22)
was critical of others	is tolerant of others (Ephesians 4:2)
complained	gives thanks (1 Thessalonians 5:18)
was involved in sexual sin	is cleansed and pure (1 Corinthians 6:11)
cursed others, wanted revenge	loves and blesses enemies (Matthew 5:44)
was proud	is humble (1 Peter 5:5–6)
compromised	takes a stand (Psalm 107:2)
was full of turmoil and tension	is full of peace (Philippians 4:7; John 14:27)
was rude to others	is gentle and kind (Colossians 3:12–13; Philippians 4:5)
was always depressed	rejoices (Romans 8:28; Philippians 3:3; 4:4)
had lustful thoughts	has the mind of Christ (1 Corinthians 2:16)

never sought God	enjoys God's presence (John 4:23–24)
kept grudges	forgives (Ephesians 4:32)
was fearful and worried	trusts in God (Psalm 91:1–2)
gossiped	builds up others (Ephesians 4:29–31)
was jealous	rejoices in others' blessings (Romans 12:15)
feared witnessing	is as bold as a lion (Proverbs 28:1)
lied and deceived others	speaks the truth (Ephesians 4:25)
was selfish	delights to do God's will (Psalm 40:8)
loved to party	lives uprightly (Romans 13:12–14)
was full of sin	is the righteousness of God (2 Corinthians 5:21)
called attention to self	calls attention to Jesus (Colossians 1:18)
was always impatient	puts up with others' faults (Colossians 3:13)
was open to the devil's ideas	gives no place to the devil (Ephesians 4:27)
dishonored parents	honors parents (Ephesians 6:1–3)
was lazy	works hard to glorify God (Colossians 3:23)
hated God	loves God (1 John 4:19)
lived in bondage	is free in Jesus (2 Corinthians 3:17; Isaiah 61:1)
was rebellious	submits to authority (Romans 13:1–4)
was stubborn	is willing to yield to wisdom (James 3:17)
was nosy about others' business	minds my own business (1 Peter 4:15)
broke promises	keeps my word (1 Corinthians 4:2; Psalm 15:4)
neglected God's Word	desires God's Word (1 Peter 2:2–3)
wanted recognition and praise	needs only God's approval (1 Corinthians 4:3–4)
was sarcastic	speaks the truth in love (Ephesians 4:15)
stole things	gives instead of takes (Ephesians 4:28)
was quick-tempered	is slow to anger (James 1:19)
used people	esteems others more than self (Philippians 2:3–4)
was bossy and demanding	is a servant (Galatians 5:13; 1 Corinthians 9:19)

RECOMMENDED READING LIST

EVANGELISM

Chantry, Walter J. *Today's Gospel: Authentic or Synthetic?* London: Banner of Truth Trust, 1970.

Coleman, Robert E. *The Master Plan of Evangelism.* 2nd ed. abridged, New Spire ed. Grand Rapids: Spire, 1994.

Comfort, Ray. *Hell's Best Kept Secret.* Expanded ed. New Kensington, Pa.: Whitaker House, 2004.

TESTIMONY

Green, Melody, and David Hazard. *No Compromise.* Eugene, Ore.: Harvest House, 1996.

Ten Boom, Corrie. *The Hiding Place.* With Elizabeth and John Sherrill. Grand Rapids: Chosen Books, 2006.

Wilkerson, David. *The Cross and the Switchblade.* With John and Elizabeth Sherrill. Grand Rapids: Chosen Books, 2000.

MISSIONS

Andrew, Brother. *God's Smuggler.* With John and Elizabeth Sherrill. 35th anniversary ed. Grand Rapids: Chosen Books, 2001.

Baumann, Dan. *Imprisoned in Iran.* Seattle: YWAM Publishing, 2000.

Cunningham, Loren. *Daring to Live on the Edge: The Adventure of Faith and Finances.* New ed. Seattle: YWAM Publishing, 1992.

Cunningham, Loren. *Is That Really You, God? Hearing the Voice of God.* With Janice Rogers. 2nd ed. Seattle: YWAM Publishing, 2001.

Elliot, Elisabeth. *Through Gates of Splendor.* Carol Stream, Ill.: Tyndale House, 2005.

Esther, Gulshan. *The Torn Veil: The Best-Selling Story of Gulshan Esther.* New ed. Grand Rapids: Zondervan, 2004.

Garlock, H. B. *Before We Kill and Eat You: Tales of Faith in the Face of Certain Death.* New ed. With Ruthanne Garlock. Ventura, Calif.: Regal Books, 2006.

Grant, Myrna. *Vanya.* Carol Stream, Ill.: Creation House, 1974.

Johnstone, Patrick, ed. *Praying through the Window III: The Unreached Peoples.* Seattle: YWAM Publishing, 1996.

Johnstone, Patrick, and Jason Mandryk. *Operation World: When We Pray God Works.* 21st Century ed. Carlisle, UK: Gabriel Resources, 2001.

Olson, Bruce. *Bruchko.* Seattle: YWAM Publishing, 2005.

Otis, George, Jr., ed. *Strongholds of the 10/40 Window.* With Mark Brockman. Seattle: YWAM Publishing, 1995.

Otis, George, Jr. *The Last of the Giants.* Tarrytown, N.Y.: Chosen Books, 1991.

Pullinger, Jackie. *Chasing the Dragon.* Ventura, Calif.: Gospel Light, 2004.

Richardson, Don. *Eternity in Their Hearts.* New ed. Ventura, Calif.: Regal Books, 2006.

Richardson, Don. *Lords of the Earth.* Seattle: YWAM Publishing, 2003.

Richardson, Don. *Peace Child.* Seattle: YWAM Publishing, 2003.

Sjogren, Bob. *Unveiled at Last.* Seattle: YWAM Publishing, 1988.

Wagner, C. Peter. *Praying through the 100 Gateway Cities of the 10/40 Window.* Seattle: YWAM Publishing, 1995.

Yun, Brother. *The Heavenly Man: The Remarkable True Story of Christian Brother Yun.* With Paul Hattaway. Toronto: Monarch Books, 2002.

MIRACLES

Wigglesworth, Smith. *Ever Increasing Faith.* New Kensington, Pa.: Whitaker House, 2001.

Wigglesworth, Smith. *Faith That Prevails.* Springfield, Mo.: Gospel Publishing House, 1979.

CULTS

Decker, Ed, and Dave Hunt. *The Godmakers: A Shocking Exposé of What the Mormon Church Really Believes.* Rev. ed. Eugene, Ore.: Harvest House, 1997.

Gomes, Alan W. *Truth and Error.* Grand Rapids: Zondervan, 1998.

Halverson, Dean. *The Compact Guide to World Religions.* Minneapolis: Bethany House Publishers, 1996.

Martin, Walter. *The Kingdom of the Cults.* Rev. and exp. ed. Minneapolis: Bethany House Publishers, 2003.

Martin, Walter. *The Maze of Mormonism.* Rev. ed. Santa Ana, Calif.: Vision House Publishers, 1978.

Mather, George A., and Larry A. Nichols. *Dictionary of Cults, Sects, Religions and the Occult.* Grand Rapids: Zondervan, 1993.

McDowell, Josh, and Don Stewart. *Handbook of Today's Religions.* Rev. ed. Nashville: Nelson Reference, 1996.

Richardson, Don. *Secrets of the Koran.* Ventura, Calif.: Regal Books, 2003.

Sire, James W. *Scripture Twisting: 20 Ways the Cults Misread the Bible.* Downers Grove, Ill.: InterVarsity Press, 1980.

SPIRITUAL WARFARE

Otis, George, Jr. *The Twilight Labyrinth: Why Does Spiritual Darkness Linger Where It Does?* Grand Rapids: Chosen Books, 1997.

Penn-Lewis, Jessie. *The Spiritual Warfare.* Fort Washington, Pa.: Christian Literature Crusade, 1998.

Pratney, Winkie. *Devil Take the Youngest.* Lafayette, La.: Huntington House Publishers, 1985.

Sherman, Dean. *Spiritual Warfare for Every Christian.* Seattle: YWAM Publishing, 1989.

Revival

America's Great Revivals: The Story of Spiritual Revival in the United States, 1734–1899. Minneapolis: Bethany House, 2004.

Bartleman, Frank. *Azusa Street.* Gainesville, Fla.: Bridge-Logos Publishers, 2005.

Brown, Michael. *How Saved Are We?* Shippensburg, Pa.: Destiny Image Publishers, 1990.

Finney, Charles. *Principles of Revival.* Compiled and edited by Louis Gifford Parkhurst. Minneapolis: Bethany House, 1987.

Penn-Lewis, Jessie. *The Awakening in Wales: A First-Hand Account of the Welsh Revival of 1904.* Fort Washington, Pa.: CLC Publications, 1993.

Ravenhill, Leonard. *Why Revival Tarries.* Minneapolis: Bethany House, 2004.

Walters, David. *Kids in Combat: Training Children and Youth to Be Powerful for God.* Lake Mary, Fla.: Creation House, 1992.

Personal Growth

Billheimer, Paul E. *Destined for the Throne.* Minneapolis: Bethany House, 1975.

Billheimer, Paul E. *Don't Waste Your Sorrows: New Insight into God's Eternal Purpose for Each Christian in the Midst of Life's Greatest Adversities.* Minneapolis: Bethany House, 1977.

Boehme, Ron. *If God Has a Plan for My Life, Why Can't I Find It?* Seattle: YWAM Publishing, 1992.

Brant, Roxanne. *Ministering to the Lord.* New Kensington, Pa.: Whitaker House, 2000.

Bridges, Jerry. *Trusting God.* Colorado Springs: NavPress, 1988.

Dawson, Joy. *Intimate Friendship with God.* Old Tappan, N.J.: Chosen Books, 1986.

DC Talk. *Jesus Freak.* Hal Leonard Corporation, 1997.

Eldredge, John. *Wild at Heart.* Nashville: T. Nelson, 2001.

Fénelon, Francois. *Let Go: Living by the Cross and by Faith.* Monroeville, Pa.: Banner Publishing, 1973.

Hession, Roy. *The Calvary Road.* Fort Washington, Pa.: CLC Publications, 2004.

Howard, Rick C. *The Judgment Seat of Christ: Including General William Booth's Vision of Heaven.* Woodside, Calif.: Naioth Sound and Publishing, 1990.

Huegel, F. J. *Bone of His Bone: Going Beyond the Imitation of Christ.* Fort Washington, Pa.: CLC Publications, 2006.

MacDonald, William. *True Discipleship.* Port Colborne, Ontario: Gospel Folio Press, 2003.

McClung, Floyd, Jr. *The Father Heart of God.* Eugene, Ore.: Harvest House, 2004.

Nee, Watchman. *The Release of the Spirit.* Reissue ed. Richmond, Va.: Christian Fellowship Publishers, 2000.

Ortiz, Juan Carlos. *Disciple.* Carol Stream, Ill.: Creation House, 1975.

Rice, John R. *Prayer: Asking and Receiving.* Murfreesboro, Tenn.: Sword of the Lord, 1980.

Wallis, Arthur. *The Radical Christian.* Revised ed. Columbia, Mo.: Cityhill Publishing, 1987.

COURSE EVALUATION

Name _____ Age _____

Date _____

Title of course completed: *Developing Godly Character*

Please answer completely and honestly.

1. What has IDC done for your walk with the Lord?

2. What was the most beneficial part of the course?

3. The least beneficial?

4. What would you change about the course?

5. Were you disappointed in any aspect of the course? Explain.

6. Please comment on the following aspects of the course. How important and valuable were they to you?

• book reports:

Continued on next page…

• missions report:

• prayer and fasting times:

• personal demands of holiness and dedication:

• amount of reading and homework:

• teachings:

• application and follow-up questions:

• Scripture memorization:

7. Please give us a brief quote about your IDC experience that we can use to advertise the course the next time it is offered.

About the Author

Vinnie Carafano lives in El Paso, Texas, with his wife, Jodie, and their four children, Vincent, Kimberly, Kristin, and Julie. He was the youth pastor of a large nondenominational church for fourteen years until God called him and his family into Youth With A Mission and King's Kids in 1993. The Carafanos currently serve as the directors of the local King's Kids base, and their ministry travels have taken them to China, India, Taiwan, the Philippines, Korea, Thailand, Ethiopia, Paraguay, Ecuador, Panama, Nicaragua, Mexico, Canada, Haiti, St. Croix, Barbados, Grenada, Jamaica, and around the United States. All four of their children are involved in various worship teams as singers and musicians.

Vinnie's lifetime commitment is to see young people come into a living relationship with Jesus Christ and affect the world around them.

About Youth With A Mission

Founded in 1960, Youth With A Mission (YWAM) is now one of the largest interdenominational Christian ministries, with 16,500 volunteer staff based in nearly 650 locations in over 130 countries. In addition, over 25,000 short-term missionaries serve each year. Coming from many different backgrounds and working in a wide range of situations, YWAMers are united in their desire to be part of changing people's lives for the better. They have responded to the Great Commission—Jesus' command to His disciples to go into all the world and tell the Good News. Because they believe that the gospel of Jesus is not just about words but is also about action, they share their faith through many different kinds of practical help—from agricultural training to running medical clinics—and tell about the Christian beliefs that inspire their actions.

Discipleship Training School (DTS) is a requirement for applying as YWAM staff and serves as a prerequisite to all other training programs. If you are exploring God's call to missions, you can use the search function at www.ywam.org to browse through YWAM locations, outreach trips, staff openings, volunteer opportunities, and even people groups that YWAM works with.

About King's Kids

Founded in 1976, King's Kids International is a worldwide youth ministry committed to leading children and teens of all nations into a proven knowledge of God and together making Jesus Christ known to all peoples in the fulfilling of the Great Commission. King's Kids equips, challenges, mobilizes, and establishes this emerging generation of young people through a partnership with the family, the local church, and YWAM. King's Kids International is a nonprofit Christian organization staffed by volunteers who, through performing arts, testimonies, sports, mercy ministry, and practical service, take thousands of teenagers each year across cultural and national boundaries to share the hope that Jesus gives. You can find out more at www.kingskids.net or kkep.org.